ANXIOUS

ANXIOUS

How to Advocate
for Students with Anxiety,
Because What If It
Turns Out Right?

LF LEAD
Forward
SERIES

**Christine
Ravesi-Weinstein**

These books are available at special discounts when purchased in quantity for premiums, promotions, fundraising, and educational use. For inquiries and details, contact us at 10Publications.com.

Published by Times 10
Highland Heights, OH
10Publications.com

Cover and Interior Design by Steven Plummer
Editing by Carrie White-Parrish
Copyediting by Jennifer Jas

Library of Congress Cataloging-in-Publication Data is available.

ISBN: 978-1-948212-20-5
First Printing: March, 2020

Dedication

This book is dedicated to Nathan and Rory, two of my life's biggest risks, and boy, did they turn out right.

Table of Contents

Foreword

I AM AN EDUCATOR and a parent. Not necessarily in that order. Throughout my career, I would pride myself on my ability to support my sons and my daughter in their academic lives. My experience as a teacher, instructional coach, principal, and district level administrator has provided me with many perspectives and skills to help them from home with their learning. Although my sons Paul and Luke either didn't need or rejected my help with school, my daughter, Allie, needed and wanted my expertise. I successfully helped her academically for years. Then high school hit.

Suddenly, her social and emotional needs were more than I could handle. It was not long before I realized the "girl drama" that I thought she was experiencing was so much more than typical. I spent hours trying to rationalize her emotions—unsuccessfully. Some days it was all I could do to get her to go to school. Because I was an educational leader, I knew what the school was thinking of my parenting skills. Her absences racked up, and the truancy letters started to come. It seemed like every night was a battle. I relied on what had been successful with thousands of students I had worked with in my career. Those strategies failed hard. I only made things worse.

Allie would perseverate on things that seemed minor, irrelevant, and even ridiculous to me. I could see how her emotions were interfering with her learning. Now our family conversations were no longer about math or reading; they shifted to social and emotional issues. Comments like: "The teacher hates me; my friend is mad at me; everybody is judging me because of what so-and-so said" sparked hours of tears. I chalked up these issues to the tribulations of high school. Until the day that changed our lives forever.

A suicide attempt landed our daughter in the hospital. After her first visit, she was discharged with a diagnosis of depression and anxiety disorder. The recommended weekly therapy visits with a counselor didn't make a big enough difference. Less than three months later, she was back in the hospital. This time, we connected with a psychiatrist who understood her triggers and had a plan for how to teach her to avoid them or cope with her episodes. Her complex plan of support included my husband and me attending classes to learn skills to help Allie cope with her anxiety. I was a well-educated woman with motherly intuitions, and I couldn't help my daughter. My husband resigned from his job so he could get her to school and be close enough to support her in a moment's notice. He and I were skeptical of what we would learn in the classes, but we faithfully attended every Saturday for twelve weeks.

What I learned in those classes changed me as a mother and an educator. I learned how anxiety works. I learned how to empathize with someone paralyzed by anxiety. I learned what I had been doing wrong and how I could be more helpful when Allie's anxiety reared its head. This new awareness of what was happening with my daughter led to more successful interactions, and significantly reduced the amount of time it took to coach her through a bad day. Not only could I recognize when she was triggered, I knew what to do—and what NOT to do. With more success under my belt, I began sharing my new set of strategies with anyone who expressed a need for them.

It surprised me how many other people close to me had been experiencing similar situations. As I shared notes with other educators in my circle, our conversations often highlighted why every educator needs to gain a new perspective on anxiety. These students are not just behaving this way for attention. Clarity about how little control individuals with anxiety have over their thoughts is not as widespread as it should be. No teacher intentionally instigates a student in emotional distress; however, when we do not comprehend clinical anxiety, sometimes our gut steers us in the wrong direction and we escalate the situation. This is why *Anxious* is crucial to the world of education.

When I met Christine Ravesi-Weinstein, I was relieved to find someone inside education who truly understands the anxious mind. She articulated the difference between a healthy brain that experiences times of anxiousness, and the physiology behind clinical anxiety that stifles its victims. She was writing articles and tweeting about her experiences with anxiety. Additionally, she offered insight into how others could help students with anxiety. Her suggestions and feedback were articulate, and more importantly—they worked! As an administrator, she had connections to hundreds of students, yet that's not enough when there are over three million teachers in the United States alone. All of them are sure to serve students with anxiety at many points in their careers. The tools to deal with anxiety are in a different box than what most of us are accustomed to using. Weinstein gives us these tools and teaches us how to use them.

Knowledge is power, and obtaining the skills to support students before, during, and after their anxiety hits is empowering. Weinstein shares how to reduce triggers for students with anxiety by being mindful of our classroom culture, carefully choosing the words we use, and being aware of the actions we take with students. Her guidance is actionable and relevant. She describes how to recognize an anxious student, identifies how that student might be feeling, and outlines ways to deescalate.

When I first became a parent, I looked at the students in my classroom differently. They were now someone else's children, and I took educating them a level more seriously. As a parent of a daughter with anxiety, I advocated for Weinstein to write this book. Teachers, administrators, bus drivers, and recess and lunchroom supervisors all encounter students who need the adults to be informed with coping strategies. *Anxious* is set to publish weeks before my Allie graduates from high school. She did not enjoy the benefit of having teachers who had learned from Christine Ravesi-Weinstein's wisdom. But your students will. You can reduce the suffering that anxiety causes your students. For the sake of everyone else's children and your peace of mind, soak in Weinstein's insight. You will be forever grateful you did—and so will your students.

— CONNIE HAMILTON, INSTRUCTIONAL STRATEGIES EXPERT, PRESENTER, AUTHOR OF *HACKING QUESTIONS* AND CO-AUTHOR OF *HACKING HOMEWORK*

Introduction
Keep Fighting

"MISS, IS THIS your train? Miss? Excuse me, Miss, is this your train?" the conductor called out as he stepped off the commuter rail and onto the platform.

I stood on the platform, nervously waiting to board my train home, and anxious for the moment when I would arrive in a less densely populated area of the state. I had just finished a long day of teaching and taking graduate classes, I was exhausted from being around people all day, and I wasn't done yet. I still had to manipulate the most public part of my day: the commute home.

"Yes," I answered, head down, ashamed, as I paced back and forth just outside of the train door. I knew I must have looked foolish, crying and talking to myself, walking this way and that, yet not going anywhere at all.

"Well, Miss, we're leaving. You getting on or what?" It was obvious the conductor didn't have time for this.

I knew what the answer was, but couldn't reply with confidence. "Yeah," I muttered, finally bolting toward the open door, the whistle blowing loudly down the track. It was a shot of adrenaline that finally launched me onto the train, a shot much like the one that had propelled me up the cellar stairs at my parents' house, after checking the laundry, for fear of the ghost down there.

I was paralyzed with fear of the train. But I had to get on. It was my only way out of the hot, humid, crowded city, my only way back home to the safety of my bedroom.

I walked through the crowded cars, looking for a seat and asking myself the same old question: "up or down?" Yet another option in my daily life. Yet another chance to choose incorrectly. I took out my cell phone and dialed my mother, who knew to wait by the phone for my nightly calls.

"Hey, honey. You getting on the train?"

"Yes, I just got on. I barely made it."

"Why are you out of breath? Did you have to run?" my mother asked.

"No, I have been waiting for a while. But I'm freaking out. I couldn't get on. Talk to me. Just distract me. I feel claustrophobic. I can't take a deep breath."

My mother didn't understand what was going on, but played along and did as requested. She talked to me about my day and school. She asked how my students were and how I did on my paper. Intermittently, she asked me how I was feeling, and if my stomach had calmed down.

My mother kept me on the line for the entirety of the ride, about thirty minutes. She succeeded in calming me, and my stomach, down, but we both knew this was a pivotal moment. It was no secret that I was high-strung, but being unable to step foot onto a train—one I had been on countless times before—was a different experience for both of us.

I was twenty-two years old when I commuted back and forth to the city every day on that train. I was getting my master's at the Harvard Graduate School of Education, while also student teaching at Snowden International High School in Copley Square. As a student, I was intently focused on perfection and success. My drive began in kindergarten and continued onward to my Harvard acceptance in the spring of 2002. I never imagined that my academic commitment was any more than the pursuit of the best education and career possible. However, at the age of twenty-two, while standing paralyzed on that platform, waiting for the train out of Boston to the southeastern suburb where I lived, I came to realize that it was more than that.

I suffered from chronic anxiety and panic disorder—and had my whole life.

I grew up the youngest of four children, and the only girl. My childhood was full of outdoor play, sports, and competitions. I was considered smart and athletic, and too intense for my own good. I had to get an A+ on every test and go ten for ten from the field; anything short of that and I considered myself a failure. There were also a few qualities about me that were a little "different": the inability to use a pen in any of my notebooks, for fear of making a mistake; the incessant rewriting of assignments before submitting them for scoring; and the chronic stomachaches that often sidelined me from social events and outings.

I assumed all those were normal experiences associated with the awkwardness of growing up. Standing, paralyzed and incapable of stepping onto a train, however, was far more intense.

To every person, what's considered "normal" is *their* normal. When I received my diagnosis at twenty-four years old, two years after that first panic attack on the train platform in Boston, I realized that for decades, I had been showing all the signs of mental illness. Yet somehow, there I was, a Harvard student and a science teacher, who never saw a therapist, in or out of school. I never took medication; I never spoke about it to a single person, including family members; and I most certainly never knew of any other student with a story like mine. My diagnosis was as foreign to me at twenty-four as the symptoms I fought at fourteen.

And I am not an anomaly. At fourteen—and before and

after—so many of our students are experiencing the *same things I did*. The fear, the uncertainty, the drive for absolute success with no roadmap for how to get there. The voices in their heads that are constantly pointing out every failure.

As educators, we must do more than just acknowledge the existence of this disease in our classrooms. We must arm ourselves with strategies for addressing it. We each will face it more times than we can count—but can we identify it? Do we know how to deal with it? What does anxiety *look* like? How can we support students struggling without exacerbating their illness? How can we advocate for these students, and help them overcome it and find success in the classroom?

I set out to share my story and experiences to help educators answer these questions and implement strategies to help students just like me.

Schools are inundated with cases of anxiety in young adults. The difficulty for educators is twofold: 1. Anxiety looks different from one student to the next, and 2. We have all been "anxious" at one time or another, so we think we understand what it is and how to overcome it. Although many students have circumstances that cause specific anxious symptoms—and are therefore easily identifiable— many of them are struggling because of their silent and debilitating anxiety. Further, one anxious moment doesn't equal deep-seated anxiety. They're two different experiences.

But how do you unearth them? And what do you do about them once you have?

Anxiety is essential for human survival. It's the basis of the fight-or-flight response that alerted our ancestors to danger. The emotional brain was, and still is, wired to be on high alert. Is there a lion about to attack? Anxiety tells us how to respond to a threat and is a function of our autonomic nervous system, which "automatically" kicks in to save our lives.

As the world we live in has changed, however, we are no longer in danger of being hunted down by predators in the bush. We have lost the *primitive* need for our anxiety. But physiologically, we are still wired to be on high alert for survival; we will always have our autonomic nervous system.

Individuals with anxiety disorders have physiologies that produce too many stress hormones—which then bathe their emotional brains each time they experience anxiety. In these students, the autonomic nervous system that is supposed to counter the fight-or-flight response never gets the opportunity to calm the person down. Their anxiety exists around the clock.

For those with "quieter" emotional brains, understanding anxiety can be difficult. As a veteran teacher, high school administrator, and mental health advocate, I see students just like me everywhere and every day; students stymied by feelings of inadequacy, competition, challenge, failure, hard work, and conflict. As a teacher, allowing mental illness to prevent students from achieving academic success is unconscionable. A vast majority of the student interventions I tackle as an administrator are for individuals with anxiety, from minor nervousness and upset to panic so crippling that students avoid school. In meeting after meeting, I listen to stories that are personally identifiable from students and families: panic attacks and stomach ailments in the mornings, late nights trying to perfect assignments, and poor test scores.

In the nearly two decades since I began working in schools, I have seen a shift in teaching and learning priorities. I began my career at a time when the biggest problems faced by our students were time management and quadratic equations. A teacher's focus at that time was academic. I taught science and prepared students for standardized tests and college admittance. I made connections with my students (personalization of student learning has always created more student buy-in and success). Still, the connections I made were about pop culture, student interests, and analogous experiences to the curriculum I taught.

Today, the biggest variable we face in our classrooms is the students themselves. They still need to learn reading and writing, math and science, communication and presentation skills. Students' abilities to learn, however, have changed. A survey published by the Pew Research Center in 2019 found that 70 percent of teenagers identified mental health as a major issue among their peers. That's a higher percentage than those who associated major issues with bullying, drug addiction, or gangs.

Until and unless we prioritize what our students see as their major issue, we're going to fail as teachers.

As educators, we must meet all students where they need us the most. Seventy percent of students believe mental health is a major issue, and we must be open-minded to addressing that. We must remove the stigma associated with mental illness and help our students address their concerns.

Students need advocates—people to be their voice during a time when they have yet to understand the language of their anxiety. Advocacy is the work and responsibility of *all* school personnel, not just support staff and school adjustment counselors. Being an advocate does not require you to suffer from the issues you champion. Rather, it requires you to take the risk and learn what it is these students need. It requires that you design a classroom culture that is safe for *all* students—even those with anxiety.

What follows are stories and strategies from both my personal and professional journeys with mental illness. As a former student, a teacher, and now a school leader, I'll speak from multiple angles and various experiences with it. As you read, you'll find stories describing real situations, followed by related strategies with hints, tips, and suggestions you can implement in your classrooms for your anxious students.

If you are ready to face anxiety head-on, help all students achieve success and personal growth, and lead others as they, too, try to tackle this difficult illness, please join me as we Lead Forward in our fight to help our students feel less anxious.

Here I am during my growing-up years in Canton, Massachusetts. I showed signs
of anxiety, but it would remain undiagnosed throughout my childhood.

I loved my security blanket, Meems.

At age twenty-three, I was living at home shortly after completing graduate school. On the outside I was very happy, yet even with therapy, I was still struggling with intense anxiety.

At age thirty-five and in my twelfth year of teaching, my anxiety was finally manageable. I was in consistent therapy, medicated, and working out. I became pregnant with my daughter later that year.

CHAPTER 1

How to Handle a Curveball

Common Missteps Educators Take in Supporting Students with Anxiety, and How to Correct Them

Be curious, not judgmental.
— WALT WHITMAN, AMERICAN POET

NXIETY IS A curious illness. Because we have all felt anxious at some point, we think we understand clinical anxiety, but the two experiences are very different. Before educators can understand what to do to support students with anxiety, they must understand why what they are already doing isn't helping. Following are stories about common missteps educators take in addressing students with anxiety, and the right steps they can take instead.

Facing Adversity

Grace was a successful high school student who made the honor roll every term and was a talented athlete. As such, her days were tightly scheduled. She spent all day taking honors and AP classes, and all afternoon at practices or games. When she got home, her mother had a meal waiting for her, and while she ate, she started her homework. After dinner, it was a shower, more studying, and then bed.

Rarely did Grace stay up after 10 p.m. She always made a point to manage her time so as not to leave assignments until the last minute. She started papers weeks in advance and reviewed tests a few nights ahead of time. Grace's success in and out of the classroom was predicated on routine and preparation. Her teachers and coaches knew her as quiet and intense.

Before educators can understand what to do to support students with anxiety, they must understand why what they are already doing isn't helping.

They didn't realize that she displayed many of the classic symptoms of anxiety.

In the spring of her senior year, Grace was well into her softball season. She played left field and led off, hitting nearly .500 for most of the season. She had a good rapport with her coach, who was her ELA teacher during her freshman year. One day, as with any home game, Grace and her teammates were balancing warmups with field preparation. While the pitchers warmed up in left field and the infielders played catch in right, Grace and the other outfielders were tasked with setting up the infield.

Grace carried the bases out to their respective spots and began placing the pegs into the preset holes in the ground. First base went in smoothly. Second base, however, was a different story. As was sometimes the case, dirt had filled the holes in the ground, and Grace was unable to get the base to lie flat. A few teammates saw

Grace struggling and came over to assist. They, too, were unsuccessful in getting the base flush. The girls began to giggle about how it would be funny to just leave the base as it was, and Coach Henderson came over to see why the girls were fooling around and the work was not getting done.

"What's going on over here? We have a game in forty-five minutes."

The girls stopped and looked at Grace, their unofficial team captain. Coach Henderson looked at Grace angrily, waiting for her reason for not following a simple, routine request.

"The base won't go in, Coach," Grace replied.

"What do you mean it won't go in?"

"There's too much dirt in the hole. The base won't go in."

"So, stick your finger in the hole and dig out the dirt!"

"I don't want to get dirty," Grace replied.

Unbeknownst to most, cleanliness was part of Grace's extreme anxiety. If she got dirt under her nail, or caked into the fingerprints in her skin, it was all she would be able to think about. It wouldn't feel right in her batting glove, and there was no bathroom with soap and running water to clean up. Having to dig out the dirt was not part of her pregame routines. If her routine was thrown off, she wouldn't have a good game.

It's similar to superstition, but it's real. The voice in her head would tell her she'd likely strikeout or make an error in the field if she followed the wrong routine. Her pregame routine was a way to control her anxiety—to curb the fears of not being good enough. If she messed it up, the voice in her head would prevail. Her anxiety would win.

"Are you kidding me?" Coach Henderson yelled.

Grace immediately started to clam up; it was in her head now. One of the major triggers for her anxiety was the fear of disappointing others. Facing her coach and his apparent disappointment inevitably caused her anxiety to build. Her heart began to race.

The voice in her head was screaming, telling her she was a failure. She was no longer focused on the game. Her anxiety was already winning.

The two stood silent for what felt like minutes, but it was mere seconds.

"Fine!" Coach Henderson said, as he bent over and dug out the dirt with his finger, grabbed the base from Grace, and stuck it into the ground. The base was flat when he stepped on it.

"Was that so hard?" he asked Grace. "I don't know why you get so worked up over stuff. Relax."

Grace stood at second base, on the verge of tears. It was the same anxiety she fought at home when her mother asked her to clean the dishes. She couldn't bear to touch the dirty sponge that sat on the edge of the sink. She could practically feel the germs crawling onto her when she touched it—just like the dirt that would have gotten under her fingernail if she'd used it as a shovel.

If she could have relaxed about the whole situation, she would have. It would have created far less awkward interactions and disappointments. But she wasn't wired that way. None of this was her choice.

Anxiety isn't always visible. As educators, we don't always know what a student is feeling or if they are struggling with anxiety. What might seem to be simple to us could be overwhelming to a student. We don't know how a student will filter our reaction in their head, and how they will respond—and we have to start taking that into account. We must think before we speak and take in the entirety of a situation before we respond. If you have students with anxiety, like Grace, you might have to change the way you interact with them.

LEAD **FORWARD** STRATEGY
Be Proactive, Not Reactive

The attention that a student's anxiety brings them can be quite anxiety-inducing in the first place. As Grace fought the fear of getting dirty, she was also feeling ashamed, even before Coach Henderson approached. From the coach's perspective, it was irrational. Grace was a star athlete, no doubt getting dirty on the softball field every day, and she was a top student; surely, she knew how to handle a little adversity. But to Grace, the situation was a lose/lose. This unfortunate yet common difference in perspectives is what leads to educators' missteps, including those by Coach Henderson, when they try to work with students who suffer from anxiety. Instead of providing effective support, educators resort to: "Was that so hard? I don't know why you get so worked up over stuff. Relax."

Students need advocates, mentors. They need educators who are more than sympathetic; they need individuals who are empathetic. If it were possible, I would give all educators anxiety for a week so they could see precisely what it is that a student with the illness experiences, but the best we can do is to give them a model for how to address these students effectively. Here are five common missteps made by educators and how you might approach them instead.

- **Ask how you can help.** Too many educators *tell* students who are anxious that it's going to be okay. Anxiety doesn't feel okay; it's overwhelming and sometimes uncontrollable. Furthermore, clinical anxiety isn't a feeling that comes out of nowhere. It's one they carry around all the time. Anxiety is panic, worry, and discomfort that still exists even when the trigger has been removed. It lives and breathes as self-deprecation, doubt, and irrationality. It's going to be okay when you're nervous for a test; the test will be over, and the nerves will be gone. Anxiety, unlike nerves, does not have a lifespan. Rather than telling a student that it's going to be okay, ask them how you can help. Be a part of the process of eventually making it all okay.

- **Relax, because they can't.** Telling someone with anxiety to relax is an easy go-to, but it's not proactive. Relaxing is exactly what the anxiety sufferer is trying to do, and telling them to relax just reminds them that they can't. This makes them feel less than perfect, like a failure, and then they are going to feel more anxious. Instead of giving directions on what they aren't able to do, redirect them on what they *are* able to do. If the educator can relax first, then the student will follow their lead. Ease into a reaction. Take in the situation, and when you feel ready, make an active suggestion as to how you might be able to help.

- **Accept that they're worried without reminding them of it.** Anxiety is all about worry. Whether the educator has already been through the situation the student is worried about, or doesn't have anxiety, they often think that telling the student not to worry will be a helpful reminder. However, it's too late. That student is already worried. Anxiety is an illness of overthinking. The internal conversations that occur ad nauseam have succeeded in making the student anxious, and the student is already begging their inner voice to breathe and not to worry. They're on it. Accept that they're worried, and be patient that with the right support, you can help them to calm down. Focus on proactive support rather than unnecessary statements.

- **Listen to what the student is telling you.** One of my biggest frustrations with educators who try to help students, but fail to do so, is when I hear them say, "Everyone gets anxious." Correct. Everyone does get anxious; it's how our emotional brains are wired. Clinical anxiety, however, is a miswiring of the autonomic nervous system. It is a physiology that is not working correctly, much like the physiology that doesn't properly produce insulin in a person with diabetes. Being anxious is healthy physiology; having anxiety is not. Telling a student with anxiety that everyone gets anxious makes them wonder even more why they're different. Rather than trying to make them feel like everyone else, simply listen to what they are telling you about how *they* feel, and consider that it's different from what your other students are feeling. Be the rational brain they need in the moment.

- **Validate their upset.** It was obvious that Coach Henderson didn't think Grace had reason to be upset, but saying that is not proactive. Telling a student, "It's not worth getting this upset about," is a reactionary comment. To a healthy individual, anxiety doesn't seem worth it; it appears to be a bad choice. First, anxiety isn't a choice. Second, for students suffering from anxiety, it is a vicious cycle of positive affirmation. If anxiety sets in, and eventually subsides without incident, the brain becomes conditioned to believe that anxiety is a means to a positive end. To someone with anxiety, it is worth it, because in the end, "it's going to be okay" if they are anxious about a situation, and it works out right. Let the student know you understand why they are upset, then help them find a solution. This approach will give both of you what you need.

Four Miles, "Easy"

In the fall of 2019, I was scheduled to run my fifth half marathon: the Boston Athletic Association (BAA) Half Marathon. In my previous four halfs, I'd failed to meet my ultimate goal: a sub-two-hour finish. My closest attempt was my first race when I finished in just over two hours and three minutes.

Image 1.1: I'm eleven miles into my first half marathon in May 2018, and ended up finishing in just over two hours and three minutes.

When I decided to run this half, I had no idea what my training would look like. When I signed up for the race as a BAA Distance Medley participant (committing to running the 5K, 10K, and Half Marathon within a given year) early in the year, a race in October was the least of my concerns.

In August of 2019, ten weeks from the race, I decided on a ten-week training program in the hope of accomplishing my goal to complete it in one hour, fifty-nine minutes, and fifty-nine seconds.

For many runners, following a training program is typical. You sign up for a race, set a goal, and pick a training program to get you there. But prior to August of 2019, I had never followed a training program for any race. Running and working out needed to feel like an escape for me, and if I followed someone else's predetermined expectations, it didn't feel like an escape. It felt like work.

The program was designed to include short runs early in the week, culminating in a long run on Sunday, each increasing in mileage as the program got further along. I quickly found that I focused my anxiety on those Sunday runs: seven miles, then eight, followed by nine miles two weeks in a row, building up to thirteen miles. I'd start to get anxious days before those long runs. Doubts would set in: that I wasn't good enough, and that I wouldn't be able to finish the run without walking. Typically, I would sabotage myself by not sleeping well the nights before.

But after the first two weeks of training, I found the runs of three to five miles to be more difficult on my anxiety than the long runs on Sunday. Then, in the third consecutive week of painful four- and five-mile runs, I realized what was happening. The training program didn't just list the length of the runs; it often listed the pace: "6 miles, 4 at 9:09 pace," "Long run, 9 miles," or "4 miles, easy."

I knew the long runs were going to be hard because they were long. But the "easy" runs should have been easy, right? Every run that was listed as "easy" became just the opposite: grueling, hard, and seemingly never-ending. They were the runs where I had to fight my head the most: *But this is supposed to be easy. Why do I feel so bad? Why is this so hard? Go easy! What's easy? Is this too easy? Maybe I should go a little faster? Are hills supposed to be easy? An easy run shouldn't be this long! If I can't do this easy run, how am I ever going to be able to finish this half marathon?*

Telling me that a run should be easy was just fuel to my anxious mind. Sure, the training program didn't know I had anxiety, but couching an assignment or activity as "easy" beforehand is a kind of death sentence for anyone with anxiety. I remember students always asking me if I thought a test was easy when I handed it out. I always answered in the same way: "It's easy to me because I am the teacher. That does not mean it should be easy for you as the student."

Educators need to be aware of the impact their opinions might have on their students, especially those who suffer from anxiety.

LEAD **FORWARD** STRATEGY
Keep Your Opinions to Yourself

Anxiety is about perfection. Trying to accomplish it all, regardless of the variables at play. Whether I should be able to run an eight-minute mile at the age of thirty-nine, after two C-sections and a surgically repaired right knee, or not, *I* believe I should. If you ask me to try, I'm going to run as hard as I can. And if I don't make it, I'm going to be disappointed, upset, and think I am not good enough.

Anxiety doesn't care about reasons. Those are just excuses. A four-mile run is going to create enough self-doubt without pre-qualifiers. If I set a goal of forty minutes, and I complete it in thirty-nine, my mind thinks: *I could have finished it in thirty-eight*. Telling me that the run should be easy before I put my shoes on is like giving my anxiety a shot of adrenaline. No effort will be good enough. I fail before I even start. My anxiety has won.

Educators need to be delicate with students who are suffering from anxiety. Too often, their efforts to build up a student's confidence serve, instead, to build up their anxiety's confidence. Anxiety feasts on an individual comparing themselves to others. Rather than sharing opinions with your students, good or bad, think instead about the mantra: Keep your opinions to yourself. Opinions are subjective conclusions. They lack sufficient evidence and often fail to take into consideration the biggest variables in the classroom: the students themselves. Opinions are shared with best intentions but can easily backfire. Rather than telling students what you think, try these strategies as you let them work at their own pace.

- **Meet those challenges.** Instead of telling a student that a task should be easy, encourage them to welcome challenges. Much like my "four miles, easy" training runs, telling students with anxiety that an assignment or skill is easy can make the work more difficult. Instead of focusing on learning the skill or content, anxious students will focus on how easy or difficult the work is for them. They're going to fixate on what "easy" means. Maybe the assignment seems easy to you, but you've already mastered the content/skill. Students may have found it easy in the past, but those who found it difficult probably didn't tell you about it. Easy is relative, and just an opinion. You might share that opinion, thinking it will calm the students' nerves, but for students with anxiety, it exacerbates them. Instead, tell students that it's okay if it is challenging. Remind them that you are there to support them and help them achieve success. Let them know that if it's not a challenge, that's great. You will support them by finding a skill or content that is more challenging.

- **Stay positive.** Rather than telling students they can do better, let them know you are proud of their work. Perfection is 100 percent, a 4.0, batting 1.000. Unless students with anxiety are perfect, they think they can do better. In fact, for many students with anxiety, the fear of imperfection drives their work and their school avoidance. These students would rather not do the work at all than do it imperfectly. If you think a student with anxiety can do better, they have already thought of it.

Saying it is only going to make them feel like they have disappointed you. At that point, it becomes unlikely that they will do better since they are crippled by the fear of not making you proud. Instead, stay positive and let students know you are proud of what they've already done, even if they have more to do.

- **Encourage the right pacing.** Self-pacing is a form of self-advocacy. Too often, I hear educators tell students ahead of an assignment or test that they should have plenty of time to complete the work. For students with anxiety, one of the most challenging aspects of test-taking is the other students in the room, because they provide a focus for the anxious mind. No matter where a student with anxiety is on a test, as soon as that first student stands up to submit their exam, the anxious student feels like a failure. The inner dialogue focuses on how their classmate is already done, why they aren't yet, and how it must mean they are going to fail. We've already talked about the way teachers can set expectations, so you already know how a student with anxiety is going to react to the statement that they'll have plenty of time to complete the quiz you've just handed out. They will decide that if they are out of time, it's because they're not smart enough. This negative self-talk is happening in the anxious mind all day, every day. These students can do without any reminders or reasons to compare themselves to others. Instead, encourage students to work at a comfortable pace. If they need to take a break for a minute, that's fine. For me, sometimes I need to stop and walk for a minute because keeping up a running pace just isn't comfortable. Remind your students with anxiety that they can walk for a little, and that it's okay to do so if it helps them keep moving forward.

MOVING FORWARD

We've gone over critical—and common—missteps in this chapter, and there's a good reason for that. Though educators take these steps with good intentions (usually), these actions fail to normalize anxiety and instead increase the isolation and loneliness felt by those with the disease. If Grace was suffering from diabetes and stood at second base going into shock, would Coach Henderson say to her, "It's going to be okay. Just make insulin. Don't lose consciousness. Everyone gets a sugar high. It's not worth stressing over"?

Of course, he wouldn't.

We all understand that diabetes is a physiological illness and that the diabetic is not in control. Educators need to hold the same understanding about anxiety. They need to approach it as the physiological illness that it is: the body's inability to produce the correct amount of neurotransmitters in the brain.

Trying to anticipate potential sticking points for students with anxiety can also be more detrimental than helpful. Explaining to a student with anxiety that an assignment should be easy or that a test shouldn't take that long—although it may be an honest attempt to be proactive and eliminate potential anxieties—increases negative self-talk.

So what could Coach Henderson, or any other educator, have done differently with a student/player like Grace? In the coming chapters, I give you stories and strategies to help educators support and advocate for students with anxiety. The differences between teachers' good and bad interactions are often subtle, but the benefits of the "good" are invaluable. The goal is to prevent the internal struggles that students like Grace experience in silence day in and day out, even amidst all their success. Take the risk to change your perspective on anxiety; what if it turns out right?

THINK **ABOUT** IT

1. Can you recall a time when you were impatient with a student? What could you have done differently?

2. What do you vow to no longer say or do because you see that it could be harmful to students with anxiety?

3. What can you say to students, or do for them, that will have a positive impact on their lives inside and outside of school?

CHAPTER 2

Observe, Ask, and Implement

Ways to Support Students in Overcoming Their Own Anxiety

Nothing in life is to be feared, it is only to be understood.
— MARIE CURIE, PHYSICIST, CHEMIST, AND NOBEL PRIZE WINNER

TWENTY FIRST CENTURY EDUCATION is all about teaching skills, not just content. As educators, we have an obligation to teach the whole student. Often, the most teachable moments happen outside of the curriculum, and working with anxious students is no different. It is in these teachable moments that educators must take a step back and "teach" students how to help themselves. This begins with assessing the situation and asking the right questions. Let the students tell you what they need. In this chapter, we will explore strategies that will help educators support students and show students how to advocate for themselves.

A Shoulder to Cry On

Mr. Franklin was a veteran staff member, well-liked, and an effective instructor. He taught ELA to juniors, both college preparatory and honors courses. Although he didn't have close relationships with all of his students, he was rarely at odds with anyone, and students never spoke negatively about him. It was evident to Mr. Franklin's students that he cared about them.

Typically, Mr. Franklin had a good read on his students. He knew who they were academically and personally. The collaborative nature of the department at his school meant that teachers knew how students interacted in many of their classes. When teachers got their rosters in August, they talked about who was who and what to expect.

Lisa was a quiet, smart young woman with what her teachers concluded was an intense drive. She was at the top of her class and a star athlete. She was known as volatile and high-strung, and her coaches often talked about it. In the classroom, though, she was typically reserved, focused, and even-keeled. She was never loud or disruptive, nor silent and emotional. She participated in class discussions and always complied with teacher requests. Any other behaviors would have been out of the ordinary.

One particular day, as students filed into Mr. Franklin's English III Honors class, Lisa had her head down and was not engaging with any of her classmates. It was different, but not worrisome. As the students took their seats and Mr. Franklin gathered his materials, the bell rang.

"Good morning, everyone."

"Morning, Mr. Franklin!" replied the majority of the class.

"Please take out your vocabulary books and study for today's quiz," he requested.

The students took out their vocabulary books and began rifling through the pages while Mr. Franklin walked through the room, engaging with students and asking if they needed any help. As he did so, he noticed Lisa crying quietly at her desk. No one was talking to her, and it was obvious that she was trying to hide her emotions. Her head was resting on her hand as she covered her eyes with her fingers.

Mr. Franklin became immediately concerned. Lisa had her vocabulary book out but was not making any ground with studying. He was unsure what, if anything, he could do. He had never seen a student just sitting and sobbing at their desk. Given her swollen eyes and red face, this had not just come on; she had been crying for quite some time.

After giving the students five minutes to review, Mr. Franklin began administering the quiz. "Alright. Please put your books away and take out a writing instrument. You will have as much time as you need to finish the quiz, but it shouldn't take you more than fifteen or twenty minutes. If you have any questions, raise your hand, and I'll come over to help."

What is not a big deal to one person might be a big deal to another—not just because they are immature kids, but because anxiety is a spiraling thought process that feels inescapable.

The class became chatty as the students put their books away and got ready for the quiz. Mr. Franklin took particular notice of Lisa, who was sniffling and wiping back tears as she put her book on the ground and placed her pen in the pencil holder. She was still not showing her face.

"Everyone ready? Okay, I'm passing out the quiz."

Mr. Franklin gave every student a quiz, including Lisa. When he arrived at her desk, she didn't look up or speak. He slid the quiz on her desk, tucking it just under her elbow so it didn't slide onto the floor. Once the students were working quietly, he went back to his desk on the opposite side of the room.

It would have been an opportune time for Mr. Franklin to get his own work done, but he couldn't stop watching Lisa. She wasn't writing on her quiz; she just kept crying. If that continued, he knew she wouldn't finish the quiz in the time provided—or do well. He could just let it be ... or he could try to help.

He got up and went to the adjoining classroom door to talk to his neighbor, Mr. Shaw, Lisa's former freshman basketball coach, and someone who knew her well. He asked Mr. Shaw to watch his class, then went back into the room and approached Lisa.

"Hey," he whispered. "Why don't you leave your quiz here and come with me?"

Without any pushback, Lisa got up and walked out of the room behind Mr. Franklin. He realized there was a risk in removing her from class since it could draw unwanted attention, but the reality was, everyone had already seen she was not well.

He led Lisa the short distance down the hallway to the school library. Once there, he went to the back of the room and found an unoccupied area. After finding seats for them, he looked at her.

"What's going on? Is everything okay?"

Lisa, still with her hand covering her eyes, began to tell Mr. Franklin, between sobs, that the night before she had been the only senior, out of three, not named a captain on next year's basketball team. She went on to explain that she'd been crying all night and all morning. To clarify, Mr. Franklin asked if she was crying in any of her classes, to which Lisa said she was.

"Did any of your other teachers talk to you?"

"No."

Mr. Franklin sat quietly and listened as she explained how hurtful the decision had been and how neither her teammates nor her coach had mentioned it to her. Lisa wanted to stay home, but her mother wouldn't let her. Mr. Franklin knew he needed to help Lisa calm down and focus on one thing at a time.

"What can I do to help you right now?" he asked.

"Nothing, really," Lisa replied.

"Do you want to try to take your quiz today?"

"Can I take it at the end of the day?"

"Sure, of course you can," he obliged as he provided her with a tissue he'd gotten from the table next to them.

"Let's breathe together, and when you're ready, we can go back to class, okay? Do you want me to talk to your coach for you? Or even Coach Shaw?"

After another few minutes, Lisa allowed that he could talk to Coach Shaw. Mr. Franklin got Lisa to smile and walked her back to class. Unbeknownst to him, their conversation had taken up a majority of the period, but seeing Lisa walk into class without her head hanging made him feel like it was time well spent.

Lisa was a student-athlete struggling with severe anxiety. Sure, being the only one of three seniors not named a captain would have been upsetting to any student, but Lisa's reaction was not typical. The disappointment was unmanageable to her because it supported the voice in her head that was telling her she wasn't good enough.

Still, this story is less about Lisa than it is Mr. Franklin, a teacher from whom we can all learn. Mr. Franklin took many right actions, not the least of which was refusing to ignore the obvious distress his student was experiencing. For many educators, a situation like this can be overwhelming. But what good was Lisa to anyone in class, including herself? Mr. Franklin took a risk in pulling her out of the classroom, but it paid off. He let Lisa gain back the control she felt she'd lost since the announcement of team captains. He asked her the right questions to help her unload her burden.

Educators can learn a lot from the actions of Mr. Franklin. Here is how you can apply this approach with your students.

LEAD **FORWARD** STRATEGY
Question What You See

Anxiety is a "quiet" illness; it's neither physical nor always visible. Additionally, symptoms can be different from student to student, and from day to day. Because of this, anxiety falls victim to perception. Lisa's panic attack because the vote made her feel lonely and like a failure, might have appeared to be an overreaction to a disappointment. Remember Grace's anxiety about placing second base in the ground before her softball game? The situation from Coach Henderson's perspective was irrational, but to Grace, it was a lose/lose and also the result of her anxiety.

From the start, educators can support students with anxiety by understanding that the situation may not be as it seems. What is not a big deal to one person might be a big deal to another—not just because they are immature kids, but because anxiety is a spiraling thought process that feels inescapable. It's not about getting their finger dirty, or about being named captain. It's about the intense fear of failure, inadequacy, lack of control, disappointing others, and not being good enough. But before educators can understand where a student is coming from or what they are going through, they must do what Mr. Franklin did.

- **Observe.** It's easy to turn a blind eye to scenarios in the world that make us uncomfortable. Life is demanding, and we are all busy with our day-to-day lives. But we can still notice what's most important within the hectic environment of education. Schools cannot be places where individuals are focusing only on what they need to do. Educators are tasked with teaching students, but teaching can't happen until we take care of the students' social and emotional well-being. Educators need to notice when something is "off." Students with anxiety need educators like Mr. Franklin, who not only notice when they are struggling, but are willing to intervene. Mr. Franklin saw a top student avoiding her work and crying at her desk. This was enough for him to step in. Observing has to be the first step if any effective strategies are going to follow.

- **Ask questions.** Just seeing that there's an issue that is not right is not enough. Mr. Franklin didn't just notice that Lisa wasn't well; he took action and asked questions to figure out what to do next. He didn't just see a problem and formulate a solution. He made the student part of that solution. Once you see a student struggling, ask questions like:

  - **Can you tell me how you're feeling?** Even if the way a student is feeling is obvious to you, asking them how they feel empowers the student to speak up and take back a sense of control a power that, when lost, causes anxiety. Also, their answer to the question will provide you with more insight into the student's struggles.

  - **What do you think might be going on for you right now?** Clinical anxiety isn't a feeling that comes on because of one specific, identifiable reason. One issue might trigger anxiety, but typically, anxiety is panic, worry, or discomfort that sets in out of nowhere. When it does become debilitating, sufferers are left feeling powerless. When you ask a question like this one, you can help the student initiate a thought process to regain control over the situation, *and* educate you about a potential solution.

- **What do you need from me?** No one likes to be told what to do, especially when it's unsolicited. But everyone appreciates an offer of help or assistance. Surveying the needs of others and selflessly asking what it is they need from you is a sign of a great leader or "captain." Expect that the student will most likely answer, "I don't know," or "Nothing," but don't read into it. They are not being unappreciative of your show of support. Ultimately, they need exactly what you're doing.

Mr. Franklin succeeded in helping Lisa without intense intervention. He began by asking Lisa two crucial questions: "What's going on?" and "Is everything okay?" He didn't draw attention to Lisa's upset by mentioning any specifics. Instead, he simply listened. He allowed Lisa to say what was going on and why she felt the way she did, without passing judgment or justification—two behaviors that could have minimized Lisa's emotions.

Mr. Franklin then asked Lisa what he could do to help. He didn't give her unsolicited advice. He allowed her to dictate her needs, providing her with an opportunity to regain control. He made suggestions that were tangible and comfortable: "Do you want to try to take your quiz today?" "Do you want me to talk to your coach for you? Or even Coach Shaw?" Lastly, he supported Lisa by engaging in his suggestions with her: "Let's breathe together, and when you're ready, *we* can go back to class, okay?" By doing this, he took away the feelings of isolation and loneliness that come with anxiety.

There's a reason that observing and asking questions are the first two steps of the scientific method. We can't possibly make a guess, even an educated one, about the likely cause of an occurrence unless we ask questions about what we are observing. Only then can we design an intervention, assess its degree of success, and make a plan moving forward.

It's a Marathon, Not a Sprint

In the summers between my years in college, I worked for a fulfillment company. The job was straightforward. The company would be contracted to complete mailing jobs and quality control inspections for other companies. The size of the job on any given day dictated the number of employees working. Sometimes we would be tasked with a large mailing or a packaging and shipping project, but mainly we did quality control inspections for Reebok.

The work itself wasn't hard. We would look at a pair of shoes, and based on a set of criteria, classify the shoes as either good—A, or bad—B. The A sneakers would go to retail stores for full price, while the Bs went to stores that sold them for a reduced price. What made the work difficult for me, and my anxiety, was the size and monotony of the various jobs. We would sometimes be presented with fifty thousand pairs of sneakers, boxed in cases of twelve pairs, and then on pallets with twenty to twenty-four cases.

The bosses would bring over a pallet, and I would start my work. The pallet would seem huge, the towering stack of shoes often so high I couldn't see over it. I would put on my music and start working through each case, one at a time. As I worked my way down the pile, I would loosen up, feeling energized that I'd be done soon. But inevitably, before I could complete the pallet, when I got to the last row of cases, my boss would come over with a new pallet. He'd place the last few cases on top of the new pallet ... and my accomplishment was gone.

Every time he did this, my breathing got shallow and my heart started to race. I often found myself fighting back tears of frustration. I would catch myself looking across the warehouse at the endless pallets of shoes, hoping I could see an end nearby.

It was the hardest physical job I ever had, but it was the least accomplished I ever felt. My anxiety had a field day. I was never allowed to finish a task; it was just day after day of the same monotony. For my anxiety, it was torture, like running on a treadmill for hours without any calculation of distance or time, and no perspective of when I would be done.

As an administrator, I see lots of Individualized Education Plans asking teachers to chunk large assignments into smaller tasks for students. This is an effective special education strategy, but it is also effective for students with anxiety. What I should have done while working at the fulfillment company is set my own goals—but not surprisingly, I didn't know how, or that I should. My well-being was in the hands of the people running the warehouse, the teachers, if you will, and they weren't any wiser.

Educators must find a way to help anxious students feel like they are making progress along the way. They have to find a way to make those pallets more manageable and the reward more immediate.

LEAD **FORWARD** STRATEGY
Set Small, Attainable Goals

Anxiety does not just affect students for a short time. Once diagnosed, they have it for life. Anxiety is a marathon, not a sprint. Students with anxiety can't expect to wake up in the morning and run across the finish line. They have to work up to the end goal. The only way to do that is by setting small, attainable goals. Each small goal is a building block for the next. With each goal a student accomplishes, they can see their growth and progress. They can feel that they're working toward a greater end result.

The journey is not about getting rid of anxiety; it's about learning how to manage it. Every day brings new triggers and symptoms. Overcoming each of these constitutes the smaller, attainable goals on which we need students to focus. As an educator, you need to not only recognize anxiety, but also figure out how to help students cope with it. Teach them to set smaller goals to increase the likelihood that they will overcome their illness and find success in the classroom. Use the following strategies to help break down large tasks into those small, attainable goals.

- **Implement the fifteen-minute rule.** Anxiety sufferers want perfection. Facing the reality, or fear, of imperfection often brings on heightened bouts of anxiety. When in a panic, students can't see beyond where they need to be, even if it's 26.2 miles away from where they are. Educators need to tap into their expertise and wisdom to help students focus on smaller goals, so they don't become overwhelmed by the bigger picture. Perfection is not possible, but trying to communicate that to someone suffering from anxiety doesn't register. Break the task up for the student. Start by saying, "I want you to focus on *this*." Once they have a focus, tell them, "In the next fifteen minutes, try to accomplish *this*." Redirecting their attention will help reduce anxiety, normalize it, and allow the student the opportunity to provide input. It's a way to help them regain control over their mind. Chunk it up in parts, not all at once, to make the tasks seem smaller. Make sure to check back with them after the fifteen minutes. Once you do, recalibrate and tell them to focus on a new task.

- **Draft a to-do list.** No matter what age you are, life is a high-maintenance proposition. As the responsibilities pile up, the anxiety increases. Once students realize they cannot accomplish all 26.2 miles on their first run, they will begin to see the power and importance of prioritization. Show them how to write a to-do list and explain how it's going to work. First, have them list all the tasks they need to do. Then have them prioritize the list, either by numbering it or rewriting it in order of what needs to happen first. Once they have finished a task, tell them to cross it off the list. Doing this can be a way to feel accomplished. I still find crossing an item off a list to be a great feeling. *One less thing*, is what I always tell myself. Making a to-do list is an indirect way of asking students to think about what they can do in the next fifteen minutes to help get them through the discomfort of their immediate anxiety; it's a great place to start.

- **Conduct a check-in.** Dealing with anxiety is not a one-time occurrence. It's chronic, and students who struggle will do so again and again. Just because they overcome one obstacle doesn't mean they won't run into another down the road. Similarly, an educator might successfully talk an anxious student through one situation ... just to find later that the student hasn't acquired long-term coping mechanisms. It is essential that educators check in with students the day after intervening during an anxious episode. A check-in can include asking the student to show their to-do list. Additionally, it can include asking them where their anxiety is today on a scale of one to ten. Make sure to ask them if it's an improvement from how they were feeling the day before. A check-in can include a follow-up on any other resolutions you worked on with the student, or a simple "Hey! How are you today? Anything I can help with?" Checking in with students makes them feel less alone. It also helps you later when it comes to observing changes in their behavior.

MOVING **FORWARD**

Much like any other major lifestyle change, **rewiring an anx-ious mind takes time and practice.** Educators must be willing to commit to making students part of the evolution of their own coping strategies. To do this, enact specific steps: observe, ask, and then implement. Observing changes in student behavior will tell educators when they need to intervene. Asking anxious students questions as a way to gauge where they are will help you develop the small, manageable goals that will inevitably help anxious students move past their difficulties. Mr. Franklin was successful in doing all three: He observed Lisa struggling, asked her questions, and developed a plan to move forward by talking to a teacher with whom she was comfortable and taking her quiz at a later time. If I had been taught these strategies at an earlier age, the work I did at the fulfillment company wouldn't have been so emotionally excruciating. But this is why educators who are advocates for students with anxiety are so important: they arm students with the coping skills they need in and out of school, and these skills will serve them for a lifetime.

THINK **ABOUT** IT

1. Do you remember a time when someone was supportive of you? What did they do?

2. What can you say to students to be supportive?

3. How can you help students focus on small goals in addition to long-term endeavors?

CHAPTER 3

Take Them by the Hand

Build Lifelong Skills with and for Students with Anxiety

Life loves to be taken by the lapel and told:
"I'm with you kid. Let's go."
— MAYA ANGELOU, AMERICAN POET

O NE OF THE biggest challenges for educators as they work with students is managing their ever-growing need for independence. It starts at a tender young age. The terrible twos are rooted in the stubbornness of independence, and the toddler must do it all on their own. This attitude never changes in most children; it simply looks different. Rather than throwing their shoes across the room because they insist they know which foot each one goes on, they skip classes because that is what will curb their anxiety about their ability to perform with perfection. But teaching is all about showing students *how*. Educators must find a way to show them where they need to be, even if they are resistant.

In this chapter, we will explore ways in which educators can show students how to cope with assignments and/or situations that are overwhelming. It isn't just about intervening; it's about taking our students with anxiety by the hand and building lifelong skills with and for them.

Pace Yourself

Ms. Callahan had been teaching AP Biology for nearly ten years. She always struggled to provide her students with an adequate final assessment, given that they all took the College Board AP exam in May. The AP exam was a comprehensive assessment that would test all of the students on the content and skills acquired over nine months. Unfortunately, Ms. Callahan would not have access to student scores before the end of the year. Ms. Callahan hated the idea of giving her students a final exam since it would mean taking two high-stakes exams a month apart. Additionally, she would rather "test" her students on the scientific skills she found valuable over the biology content she taught.

After numerous attempts at designing a quality final assessment, she decided to give it one more try. Instead of worrying about the breadth of the content covered over nine months, she decided to focus on real science: inquiry-based lab design, experimentation, and analysis.

With each unit of study, Ms. Callahan had the students spend a week in the lab. She provided students with a question and then they worked in groups to complete research, devise a testable hypothesis, design and conduct an experiment, gather data, analyze outcomes, and make a conclusion. Ms. Callahan provided a rubric for the students' presentations. Because each lab was different, students would present what they did and be scored on their lab work and presentation. This was the basis of the scientific skills the students worked on all year.

For this year's final exam, Ms. Callahan opted to assign one last lab: a full inquiry-based lab design on plants. Maintaining the same expectations, she asked students to come up with their own questions and make a final presentation on their work. It was essentially a science fair project. Other than using the same scoring rubrics and being required to work with plants, the students were free to choose their own projects. They needed to collect at least two weeks of data, and that was it. Ms. Callahan assigned the project in March, which gave the class plenty of time to prepare, design, conduct, analyze, and present their work at the end of May. She explained that she wanted all questions run by her, so she could make sure everyone was doing projects that were different, scientific, challenging, and safe.

The AP exam was approaching, and Ms. Callahan started using the final two weeks to review and study, assuming that the students were well into their plant labs. She provided a weekly agenda on which the due date appeared, and gave verbal reminders at the end of every class.

On the due date, she was eager to see the students' presentations. As groups showcased their work, she was pleased with what she saw. Except for errors in units and missed calculations, the work was impressive; the students sounded like real scientists. Aside from making minor changes, she felt this was the final exam for which she'd always hoped.

At the conclusion of the presentations, Ms. Callahan asked if all the students had participated. With no one indicating they had yet to present, Ms. Callahan considered the project complete and the assignment a success.

As she went through her rubrics and entered scores, however, she realized that Jared's name was not on any of the papers. For a moment, she was concerned that he had not participated, but he was an AP student, so surely he'd done part of the work. Jared had struggled to keep up with the work all year, but with his final grade dependent upon completion of the exam, there was no way he would have skipped it.

The following day, as the students arrived for their final class, Ms. Callahan caught Jared in the hallway.

"I didn't see your name on any of the rubrics, and I don't remember seeing you present. Which group were you a part of?"

"I wasn't," Jared replied.

"Did you do a lab on your own?"

"I started to."

Ms. Callahan was getting concerned. "Did you finish?"

"No."

"Jared, this project counts as your final exam grade. It's a big deal. Do you have anything to turn in?"

"No."

"You're going to take a zero?" Ms. Callahan was confused; she'd never dealt with a situation like this before. "You know this is going to have an impact on your final grade, right?"

"I know."

"I really wish you'd mentioned it to me sooner, Jared, I could have helped you. I'll calculate your grade and hope this doesn't affect you too negatively."

Jared just shrugged and put his eyes to the floor, refusing to make eye contact with Ms. Callahan. When she was done, he walked away and headed into the classroom. Ms. Callahan glanced at a colleague about ten feet away and put her hands up.

"He didn't do his final. AP student."

What Ms. Callahan failed to recognize was that the trouble had started long before that final lab was due. Jared suffered from anxiety that presented in the form of work avoidance. The struggle to keep up with work all year, which Ms. Callahan had noticed, had been a missed opportunity for her to intervene or figure out what was going on. By the time she presented the final assignment, Jared was so riddled with anxiety that he chose to avoid the work entirely.

When Jared found himself with a failing grade, administration got involved. Ms. Callahan explained that she reiterated due dates for weeks in advance, but administration had further questions. Had she pared down the work to help students with pacing? Had she given them checkpoints along the way to provide adequate and valuable feedback? The project was top-notch, but its implementation needed work. Ms. Callahan needed to check for understanding along the way. If she had, she would have found out what Jared was doing long before the final project was due. She could have kept his anxiety from impacting his final grade. Because they couldn't determine whether Jared had actually understood the material or the assignment, they asked Ms. Callahan to provide him with a second opportunity. She obliged, and Jared passed the course.

LEAD **FORWARD** STRATEGY
Change Approaches, Not Expectations

We are all likely to see a student like Jared in our classrooms, if we haven't already. While educators will continue to assign projects with high stakes or that require weeks, or even months, of work, they need to approach large assignments differently. Educators are facilitators and mentors for student growth. Show students how to be successful so they can model our example. Students with anxiety need even more guidance. Just starting an assignment can take hours or days. Being able to rely on scheduled help along the way will help anxious students be less work-avoidant.

Anxiety is an illness that does not discriminate; it impacts students of all academic abilities. In fact, it's the anxious students in the Honors and Advanced Placement courses that often go the most unrecognized. Sometimes we assume that academic success means anxiety doesn't exist. However, it can be the exact opposite: academic success *means* high anxiety. Many educators take the academic success of our students, a weighted GPA, an SAT score, or a class rank, to be the sole focus of student achievement. But for many students, the emotional investment necessary for accomplishing these goals is where the real story begins. How many times did Johnny start, delete, and restart his *Hamlet* essay? How many hours did Jose spend studying for his unit test in World History II? How many times did Hannah rewrite her notes to get them just right? How many times did Jared try to start his plant lab, but stop because he was overcome with anxiety?

Whether or not students are in AP classes, they must learn to avoid triggers if they're to manage their anxiety. If they are inclined to skip work that seems like it will induce anxiety, they look at the scale and scope of a task, and rather than alter their approach, choose to eliminate the need to do it altogether. Jared knew the importance of his final lab but was so anxious about failing it that emotionally, it was easier not to do it. This is known as avoidance. Educators can keep assigning such projects to all students, including anxious students. As we've seen, telling them they don't have to do that assignment just encourages the anxiety. But to make it more palatable for students with anxiety, here are a few alternatives to consider when it comes to teaching better habits to students, and keeping them from avoiding the work.

- **Refuel in pit row.** Even the highest-performing stock cars need to make pit stops before finishing a race. During the Indianapolis 500, an IndyCar makes, on average, five stops. Of course, many variables go into the number of pit stops: fuel consumption, damage, tire wear. Regardless, no IndyCar has yet to make it five hundred miles without stopping. Your students can't be expected to, either. Teach students how to pare down their work into smaller goals by replacing major deadlines with manageable checkpoints.

  Rather than only having a final due date, Ms.

Callahan should have had multiple due dates throughout. She could have started with a due date for the question students would be testing. From there, she could give the students a week to draft a hypothesis, set of material, and a procedure. She would have been able to check students' plans and give them feedback on what they wanted to do, which would have allowed students with anxiety to visualize whether their project was realistic. Ms. Callahan would have been able to help her students tease out their plan and come up with a workable procedure.

Next, she could have required students to take pictures of their set-ups. This would have ensured that students were ready to "do" the lab. Additionally, due dates could have included data collection and analysis. Then, the final due date would have been a conclusion, and by then, students with anxiety would have known whether they were doing it right. They would have known each step of the way.

Had Ms. Callahan assigned the plant lab based on these "pit stops," Jared would have been more likely to complete it. Ms. Callahan also would have been aware of his progress, or lack thereof, well before the second-to-last day of class. She could have worked to eliminate his project avoidance. Essentially, she would have created small, manageable goals for Jared to meet—and demonstrated for him how to do so. Asking your students to refuel along the way not only increases the chances that they will overcome their anxiety, but also increases the likelihood that they'll produce a quality final product.

Plant Lab – Final CALENDAR
AP Biology
Ms. Callahan

The following dates and descriptions are **checkpoints** that indicate what part of your project is due, i.e., TO BE SHARED with me (mscallahan@email) on GOOGLE DRIVE so that I can MAKE COMMENTS. I will be looking through your work to make sure that your group is on task with the assignment and have enough time to gather your minimum 2 weeks worth of data and then complete your analysis and conclusion by Senior Finals.

Monday, April 24: Presentation through and including Experimental Design/Methodology (no pictures necessary)

Friday, May 5: Presentation through and including Experimental Design/Methodology WITH PICTURES (I know it is set-up). Resolved previous suggestions.

Friday, May 19: Presentation through and including DATA WITH PICTURES (to see that your two weeks of data has been collected). Resolved previous suggestions.

Senior Final Exam Day: Completed Presentation (through conclusion) to be presented to the class.

Image 3.1: This is an example of the "pit stops" in the plant lab that would have helped students like Jared stay on track.

- **Talk with, not at, students.** Ms. Callahan thought that giving her students general, verbal reminders of due dates and expectations would be enough to keep them on top of their assignment. It's also safe to assume that she believed she was approachable: she explained to Jared that she "really wished" he'd "mentioned it… sooner," and that she "could have helped" him. But rather than leaving the decision in the hands of the students, teachers must take the initiative to make the conversation happen regularly. Engage students in frequent group conferences as a means to check in on their progress. Designate time once a week for students to check in with their groups about where their work stands.

  During this time, move through the room and talk to each group about how they're doing. Start by asking where they are with the project. Ask what the next steps are and who will be responsible for what. Offer your assistance: what can you do to help them accomplish the next steps? Let students know where you think they should be at the next check-in.

Engaging in these conversations with students will reduce their anxiety about talking to their teacher one on one. Regardless, real teaching and learning happen when students and teachers are actively engaged in meaningful conversations with each other. Talking with students is a powerful exercise.

- **"Flex" your muscles.** Students are regimented from the time they enter preschool until they graduate twelve to fourteen years later. Although routines *are* an effective strategy for students dealing with anxiety (see Chapter 9), educators have to allow students the opportunity to establish their own routines. We must think outside the box and "flex" our muscles to advocate for a new approach to scheduling in our buildings and our classrooms. Include time during the day for students to address the social and emotional needs they *all* have.

  Providing time once or twice a week for students to organize and work at their own pace will help them break down large assignments themselves. If your school doesn't have "flex" time built into the schedule, start by offering this time in your classroom. Ask students where they are with their work in your class, and how you can help them going forward. Additionally, give them feedback on work they have recently done. It will motivate them further. Creating "flex" time in your schedule allows students the opportunity to establish healthy routines and coping mechanisms during the school day. If "flex" time was part of the schedule at Ms. Callahan's school, or in her classroom, perhaps she could have offered students support on their labs, or students like Jared could have worked on the project in school.

Lend a Helping Hand

Jane had been a high-functioning young girl for years. She was entering her sophomore year of high school and didn't have any reason to believe that would change. Freshman year had come and gone with the expected amount of teenage drama. She passed all of her classes and was looking forward to returning to school in the fall. But over the summer, she changed. She started to experience intense anxiety at what she felt were odd times: before going out with her friends, when trying to fall asleep at night, and even at the dinner table with her family. The prospect of school starting again had gone from exciting to daunting; would this anxiety persist?

The school year began, and Jane's anxiety didn't subside. Instead, her panic became a relentless force in her life. Her older sister was a senior at the same school, but they were not close enough for Jane to lean on her. She also didn't want to ruin her sister's senior year. The last thing her sister needed was to be in the shadow of her little sister's anxiety.

Jane tried to be optimistic about the start of the year. She did her best to fight the anxiety she was feeling, but at times it was impossible to overcome. Without knowing what was going on, she began avoiding scenarios she knew would make her panic: a class, an interaction, an assignment. She felt it was easier just to continue fighting internally; who would understand how she felt, anyway?

But Jane's individual fight came to an end when she was called to the office for skipping a class. She knew she shouldn't have spent the class time in the bathroom, but what else was she supposed to do? Who was going to believe her when she explained that she just couldn't go to class?

Jane entered the office, and the assistant principal, Mrs. Connelly, called her in. "So, you were written up. Did you know that?" Mrs. Connelly asked.

"No."

"You didn't?" Mrs. Connelly expressed surprise.

"Not specifically."

"Did you go to math yesterday?"

"No, I didn't." Jane was embarrassed to admit the truth, but she couldn't lie about it.

"Where were you?"

"The bathroom," Jane answered.

"For the whole class?" Mrs. Connelly couldn't believe a student would spend fifty minutes or more in a bathroom rather than going to class. "Why?"

"I was feeling anxious," Jane admitted.

"Why didn't you go to the nurse?"

"I didn't feel comfortable."

"Do you get anxious a lot?" Mrs. Connelly asked.

Jane decided to tell the truth, knowing that she didn't have enough energy to keep it hidden. She told Mrs. Connelly that this had happened over the summer, and that she hadn't told anyone except her mother. Also, that she didn't think her mother understood what was going on with Jane.

Instead of telling her that it was nothing, Mrs. Connelly asked her to come to the office the next time she was feeling anxious, and offered the services of their adjustment counselors. She said they were there to help with emotions and struggles, rather than just academics. Then she offered to set up an appointment for Jane.

"All right, head back to class, and next time, come here instead of spending the period in the bathroom. Got it?" Mrs. Connelly smiled at Jane and hoped she'd lift her head to smile back.

"I got it," Jane said, as she looked up and half-smiled back at Mrs. Connelly.

The next time Jane experienced anxiety and didn't think she could go to class, Jane took Mrs. Connelly up on her offer to come

Educators must be the help that students don't know they need. It isn't just about teaching students a lesson; it's about arming them with the skills to build their own coping mechanisms later in life.

to the office. After about twenty-five minutes of quiet, Jane was able to go back to class and finish out her day.

Jane began seeing one of the school adjustment counselors and even talked to her pediatrician about her anxiety. Once Jane's anxiety and panic attacks were brought to light, she was able to attend counseling regularly.

Mrs. Connelly successfully helped Jane because she prioritized helping her, rather than enforcing the rules. Yes, it was a problem that Jane had skipped a class, but Mrs. Connelly chose to help Jane figure out *why* she skipped, rather than make the point that she would get in trouble for skipping.

LEAD **FORWARD** STRATEGY
Show Students There Is Help

Many students don't know what help is available, but we can show them and be the catalyst so they can learn their own coping skills. In a perfect world, every system, institution, and organization would run efficiently and successfully on its own. The same goes for our body systems. But it's just not always the case. Sometimes we get sick. We might try to fight the illness on our own, and sometimes we succeed, but we might also fail and have to seek a doctor or medication. The growth—in this case, the healing process—only can take shape when we admit that we can't do it on our own.

Students want to believe they are invincible even when they know they are struggling. Admitting to a weakness is difficult when you are trying to find your place in the world. Educators must be the help that students don't know they need. It isn't just about teaching students a lesson; it's about arming them with the skills to build their own coping mechanisms later in life. Show students how to find help in the following ways.

- **Introduce students to support staff.** The stigma associated with mental illness leads to a stigma on therapists and adjustment counselors. I have often found that school support staff is kept quiet for that reason. Students may know they exist only because they have friends who see them, or maybe they see them working when there is a crisis in the building. Educators need to help change that stigma by introducing these people to students at the beginning of the year. Invite them into your classrooms to help with a lesson, or include them in the staff duty schedules so they are more visible in the building. Have support staff participate in student assemblies. Make them accessible to everyone, and you will help to remove the idea that they are only available to the students who have problems. This will make it easier for students to visit them without worrying about their own reputations.

- **Plan social/emotional programming.** Historically, schools have prioritized outside programming centered on substance abuse. Although substance abuse is an important topic, schools fail to prioritize the underlying factors— including mental illness—that can so easily lead to drug use. Districts should tackle the *cause* of the abuse, so they succeed in educating students about coping mechanisms and skills for those causes. They're ignoring the anxiety and depression so many students feel and which leads them to substance abuse. We need to address this. Invite individual mental health advocates to share personal success stories, and work to develop school-based programming and initiatives. Spend time on social and emotional wellness, and you will positively impact students who suffer from mental illness. You will lead those students toward better mental health—and better academic success.

MOVING **FORWARD**

Anxiety is an exhausting battle of wills: person versus self. Couple that with the external battle all students have with the adults around them. I work with students who are desperate to be treated like the adults they think they are every day. The reality is that students with anxiety are no more in control of it than they are their own lives. Educators must take students by the hand and show them how to manage the difficulties they face.

It's even more important for students with anxiety, who need to manage the triggers in their lives.

When it comes to assignments, educators need to anticipate triggers and break up tasks into smaller chunks. Assign more than just a final due date. Pace the work out for the students and give them checkpoints and pit stops to help them build endurance when the work gets difficult. Teach the students how to do this for themselves, so they can start to manage their triggers and anxiety. Additionally, show them the supports around them; introduce them to the school support staff, and communicate to the school community that those people are there for everyone. Show students help is available by sharing survivor stories. Tell students about people who have successfully asked for help, and encourage them to do the same. Take your anxious students by the hand and show them what is possible.

THINK **ABOUT** IT

1. How would your interactions with students about their work look different if you assign checkpoints rather than due dates?

2. What would be the benefits of "flex" time in your school?

3. What would you like to see implemented at your school to expose more students to social/emotional wellness?

CHAPTER 4

Be Yourself

Use Your Own Experiences as a Guide for Anxious Students

We are the ones we've been waiting for.
We are the change that we seek.

— BARACK OBAMA, FORMER PRESIDENT OF THE UNITED STATES

NO DOUBT WE'D like to make a lot of changes in our schools, and we'd like to give more to our students. More funding, fewer standardized tests, classrooms without anxiety ... but we can't tackle it all at once. We *can*, however, offer a greater influence than we realize, just by being ourselves. Create an environment in which students see the positive outcomes of teachers being themselves, and giving students permission to be themselves as well. You might work in an underfunded school, or have to administer yet another standardized test, but be known as the teacher who is "real," and you'll have fewer students fighting anxiety just to get to class.

You'll add more value than you might realize—particularly for students with anxiety—just by being yourself in the classroom.

A Smart Risk

Ms. Walsh had been a teacher for thirteen years. She always believed there was an art and a science to her profession. Yes, she'd gone to graduate school and earned her degree, but the science of teaching was only going to get her so far. The *art* of teaching could not be taught. It was the side of teaching that came from experience, risk-taking, and passion. When friends and family asked how she didn't burn out from the sometimes grueling nature of teaching, she replied, "I tell my students: three shows a day, free admission."

Ms. Walsh needed to be a facilitator and educator, as well as an entertainer, and she also wanted to be sure she was a "real" teacher. Being real meant being relevant and approaching the skills and content from a real-life perspective. She often practiced this when introducing new content; students would rave about the relevance of her analogies and how often they changed their views of the world around them. But how relevant is too relevant? During a class on neurotransmitters and the firing of action potentials, Ms. Walsh found out.

"So as the neurotransmitters sit in the synaptic cleft after being released, they will continue to stimulate the postsynaptic neuron until reuptake occurs. This can have negative consequences on the organism's mood and behavior. Does that make sense? Does anyone have any questions? Yes, Amy?"

Amy was a student who rarely, if ever, participated in class discussions. Ms. Walsh was thrilled to see her hand raised.

"So, is this the mechanism that SSRI drugs work on?" Amy asked.

Ms. Walsh was frozen. She had a split second to make a decision; either provide Amy, and the class, with the textbook answer (yes, they regulate the uptake of neurotransmitters to stabilize mood), or give her the real answer ...

"Yes, that's how those drugs work. For instance, the SSRI drug that I am on, Zoloft, works to regulate serotonin levels in my brain and ensures that the correct amount is in the synapse after release."

"Does it work?" asked Rob.

"For me, yes, God yes, it works so well."

"So you have anxiety?" asked Amy, who had a look of shock on her face.

"Um, yeah, I do, and depression. Was diagnosed over a decade ago. That's what the Zoloft is for."

The questions continued. Students wanted to know more about Ms. Walsh's diagnosis and struggles and even began to share symptoms and fears of their own. The class never got back to the specifics of the brain—the prescribed curriculum—but the level of engagement in the discussion was the type of stuff teachers dream about.

But had she, Ms. Walsh wondered, gone too far in talking about her own experience with SSRI medications? Had she revealed too much, made herself vulnerable to repercussions?

Later that night, she received an email from Amy, thanking her for sharing her story. Amy said it had made her feel less alone about her own diagnosis. She said that Ms. Walsh had explained anxiety better than any of her doctors had been able to explain it.

After debating all day as to whether or not she'd made the right decision, Ms. Walsh was convinced that she had. She'd helped one of her students by sharing a part of herself. Even more important, she'd helped one of her students with anxiety to feel less isolated.

LEAD **FORWARD** STRATEGY
Be Authentic

Educators must take these sorts of risks in the classroom: smart risks. Great leaders share with their students and show them the path forward. Ms. Walsh's decision to tell her story of anxiety was a smart risk because she was able to reach a student with anxiety on a personal level. To be great leaders, we need to take those smart risks that put us on the same level as our students. Doing so not only shows students how to deal with a health issue, but inspires, motivates, and removes any isolation they feel. It's a way to lead forward.

Although there are certain topics you *must* temper when you are in front of your students—your language, certain details about your personal life, and your political viewpoints—you also should be able to define the inherent qualities of who you are. We are all people first, and you must show this to your students. Authenticity is key.

As stated so beautifully by John C. Maxwell, American author and leadership expert, "Students don't care how much you know until they know how much you care." Maslow's hierarchy of needs teaches us that until and unless our basic needs are met—food, water, shelter, and clothing—nothing else matters. For students today, another need that is quickly becoming a necessity is social/emotional connection.

As educational leaders, we must build positive personal relationships with students to lead them toward academic success. By being authentic, Ms. Walsh connected with not just Amy, but her entire class. It was the risk she took in giving students the relevant answer, as opposed to the textbook one, and it brought forward her authenticity and showed her students that she cared.

Students with anxiety need authentic leaders. They have to trust the person to whom they are giving control. If they can't connect with you, or don't know who you are, they are unlikely to let go of their control. They'll fight even harder to keep hold of it. Be your authentic self, and you help to build that trust—particularly with anxious students.

Consider using the following foundations of authenticity that Ms. Walsh used to create a "family" in her classroom. Her students even began using the #family hashtag when they talked about her class on social media.

- **Be compassionate.** Life sometimes gets in the way. Understand that there is more to the lives of your students than what you see in your classroom, and you'll start finding ways to increase flexibility with due dates, deadlines, and expectations. Students with anxiety are afraid of failing: a test, homework, a practice, a music lesson, a line in the school play. We need to build flexibility into their idea of success. If we were all graded on bike riding after our first attempt, we would all fail, and it's unlikely any of us would try again. Learning to ride a bike takes practice. But the goal is to learn to ride *eventually*, not in two days.

  So, if the goal in the classroom is to meet the content standard, why worry about *when* it is met? Be compassionate and flexible with your students. Ask them why they were unable to meet an expectation or deadline. Listen to what they are telling you. Tell them you understand and ask for feedback on a more reasonable expectation, given the circumstance. Work with the student rather than adding more to their plate. It's a team effort, and being compassionate is a way to bring you and the student closer.

- **Be patient.** Many people are uncomfortable with the feelings that come from unresolved issues, open-ended deadlines, and having to wait to be helped. A student's inability to meet your expectations can be infuriating. But patience is a virtue. Juggling all the responsibilities of life can be difficult for adults, and we're supposed to know how to do it.

  It's best to discover the curriculum through trial, error, revision, and retesting, and the same can be said of life. Students aren't always going to get it right the first time. Whether it's recognizing sight words, factoring an equation, or answering a Document-Based Question (DBQ), students grow and succeed only when given the time and space to do so. Teacher patience creates an authentic environment and encourages that growth.

Be patient with student progress. Ask what you can do to help them or where they are having difficulty. Tell students they have time and ask them to work with you to determine how much time they need. Patience is more than waiting; it is taking a step back and meeting the students where they are. It's not an idle strategy; it's an active support.

- **Be positive.** Positivity is contagious. Life throws many curveballs, as Grace discovered in Chapter 1, and as anxiety sets in, people tend to focus on the negative in those situations. But it's more powerful to focus on the positive. Celebrating the accomplishment of a small goal is just as important as celebrating a big accomplishment. Smile at your students. Give them a fist bump. Acknowledge their hard work before they even finish a task. Each of these teacher behaviors helps with student productivity. Furthermore, this approach is infectious and will motivate students to *want* to work because they know that any accomplishment, no matter the size, will be met with positivity.

- **Be funny.** It's been said that laughter is the best medicine. The endorphins released during laughter are similar to those released during exercise. Endorphins are "feel-good" chemicals in the brain. Using humor in the classroom can pay large dividends, not just in the long term with student success, but also in the short term. It

encourages the release of chemicals that offset the negative symptoms in an anxious student's mind. Moreover,
humor brings people together and shows real authenticity in the classroom. Laugh with your students. Let
the students joke with each other. Laugh at yourself.
Tell students funny stories. You're going to be spending
a lot of time together, and we all know that time flies
when you're having fun. Use that to your advantage.

There Is No Finish Line in the Game of Life

Ms. Walsh and Amy's connection didn't stop at the lesson on
neurotransmitters. Ms. Walsh became a "go-to" for Amy whenever she questioned her emotions or the physical symptoms she
was feeling from her anxiety. She would stop by Ms. Walsh's
office whenever she was experiencing those symptoms: shakiness,
indecisiveness, and scratching her hand so severely, she caused
herself to bleed.

Amy began asking how Ms. Walsh had freed herself from her
anxiety. Ms. Walsh explained that she was never "free" from her
anxiety. Every day, she had to manage it, and some days were
harder than others. She explained that she'd figured out how to
use outlets, and the biggest one was physical exercise. She was a
recreational runner and would alternate between going for two- to
five-mile runs and lifting weights.

"Try going for a run," she told Amy. "The high that I get from
the endorphins always makes me feel better. You ran cross country,
didn't you?"

"Yeah, but I didn't like it and I wasn't good at it."

"Oh, come on. I'm sure you are a better runner than I am. Try it again. Maybe you'll feel differently if you're doing it because you want to, rather than as part of a team. Set a date and go for it."

Amy set out for her first run three months after the conclusion of her final cross country season. She told Ms. Walsh the next day how good it felt to go for a run, and how much better she felt afterward. She began running regularly, which motivated Ms. Walsh to continue to do so, even on the days when she didn't feel like it.

Toward the end of Amy's senior year, she and Ms. Walsh began running together after school. They would set off from the school parking lot and run for four to six miles. It had always been one of Ms. Walsh's goals to complete a road race, and the two signed up for a 5K. They completed the race together, with their families watching. Amy and Ms. Walsh have since completed over twenty-five races together, including four half marathons.

Educators have feelings, fears, and struggles, too. We aren't standing in front of a class because we performed perfectly all the time. Knowing this gives students—especially the anxious ones—one more way to relate to us.

The connection that Ms. Walsh made with Amy wouldn't have happened if she had not allowed her own experiences to guide her work. What's more, if she hadn't connected with Ms. Walsh, Amy may not have realized that she could manage her anxiety—though never truly defeat it—with other activities. Because Ms. Walsh shared her struggles and coping skills, it gave Amy a safety net. Ms. Walsh normalized anxiety.

LEAD **FORWARD** STRATEGY
Normalize the Illness

Anxiety is no longer unique; it's omnipresent. But students suffering from it don't feel that way. Sharing our own experiences allows us to impact students and guide them in their paths.

Authenticity requires compassion, patience, positivity, and humor. When we're authentic, we encourage our students to pursue and acquire life skills through their own experiences. Authenticity also gives educators the tools they need to normalize anxiety and panic, and reduce the isolation anxious students feel. Practice your authenticity in the classroom with the following methods:

- **Inspire students.** Students, like many people, are often worried about what others are going to think of them. They fear missing out, and therefore try to keep up with the Joneses. Adolescence can be a difficult time of self-discovery and social acceptance as students try to balance who they are and who they want to be. When you set yourself up as an educator who is authentic and true to yourself, and not just an authority figure, you inspire students to do the same. Show students who you are. Share your relatable experiences with them. Tell them about a time when you faced adversity and were able to persevere. Ms. Walsh was able to do this for students like Amy by just being herself. She never set out to be inspirational; she just happened to be. As such, she normalized anxiety as a disease she was controlling—and that others could control as well.

- **Be honest.** When you are authentic, you are honest, which leads students to trust you and build rapport with you so they can believe in what you are teaching, in academia and in life. You also teach those students about the power of honesty. Tell them the truth when they ask. If you struggled as a kid, or still do, tell them that. They will learn more from you when they know you aren't perfect than they will if you pretend to be perfect.

- **Show humility.** Humility shows vulnerability, which shows your students that every occurrence is only one small segment of a chapter in the book of life. It opens the door to disappointment but also opens the door to success. When you allow students to see your humble moments, you make yourself more relatable—and teach students that they don't have to be right the first time, every time. Explain your challenges, not just your successes. If you graduated from an Ivy League school, tell them how hard it was. If you got suspended from school, tell them why. If you had a panic attack in Panera, admit to it. Celebrate your failures more than your successes, to normalize those failures. Students with anxiety will hear you and learn to ease up on themselves.

- **Be human.** Being authentic means being human. Educators have feelings, fears, and struggles, too. We aren't standing in front of a class because we performed perfectly all the time. Knowing this gives students—especially the anxious ones—one more way to relate to us. If you still haven't graded the tests from earlier in the week, tell them why. If you aren't going to collect an assignment, explain it. We are human, and our students are a family. Family units work when members know they care about each other and everyone's needs are met. Classrooms should be this way too.

MOVING **FORWARD**

Authenticity allows you to create a safe and productive learning environment for all students, especially those suffering from anxiety. Students with anxiety need educators who are compassionate, patient, positive, and humorous. Students with mental illness feel they can only be who they are when no one is looking, and need educators who are unapologetically themselves when others *are* looking. These educators are inspirational, honest, humble, and human. Great leaders inspire by failing forward. Share your experiences, especially if you have anxiety yourself. Teach your students through your own experiences; it is the most relevant, engaging learning.

THINK **ABOUT** IT

1. What qualities did your favorite teacher possess?

2. Name ways that you can be more authentic with your students.

3. What do you want your students to remember about you? How can you accomplish this?

CHAPTER 5

Teach the Truth about Social Media

Help Students with Anxiety Navigate a Fantasy World of Perfection

No insect hangs its nest on threads as frail as those
which will sustain the weight of human vanity.
— EDITH WHARTON, AMERICAN NOVELIST

THERE'S NO QUESTION that technology is an essential part of twenty-first-century learning. Our worlds are predicated on its successful implementation. But with every positive change we make, we must deal with a negative implication. Screen time is a legitimate concern for individual development and even more of a concern for students with anxiety, for whom social media has even bigger repercussions.

Educators must find ways to help students understand the reality of the technological world. Explain to students with anxiety that social media is a contrived reality. It doesn't mean technology is all bad, but it does tell them that social media might trigger their anxiety. Effective leaders think forward and lead in that direction.

Teach the truth about social media, and help your students with anxiety navigate the unrealistic portrayals of perfection so they can achieve their best personal success.

"Better Amy"

In Chapter 4, we met Amy, a student with intense anxiety in Ms. Walsh's biology class. Amy found a connection with Ms. Walsh after her teacher opened up to the class about her own struggles with anxiety. One of Amy's symptoms was self-loathing. She often talked about herself with intense self-deprecation. Her clothes weren't brand name; her hair wasn't straight; she didn't like her glasses.

One afternoon, while talking to Ms. Walsh, Amy mentioned how much it bothered her that she would never be like the other girls in her class.

"I'll never be Better Amy, or Jennifer," Amy explained.

"Better Amy? Please don't tell me that's how you refer to her. Come on! You have so much going for you. What do they have that you don't?" Ms. Walsh asked.

"Look at them. They're perfect. And so beautiful!"

"Perfect? What's perfect about them? And you're beautiful, too."

"They're so popular and pretty. And the boys love them."

"That's just your perception, Amy. How do you know what their lives are like outside of here? And don't kid yourself; you're pretty, too."

"Not like them. Have you seen Jennifer's Instagram? Look at the picture she posted yesterday."

Amy took out her phone and showed Ms. Walsh a post that Jennifer had made. The picture was gorgeous: Jennifer with her long, blonde hair hanging ever-so-slightly over the right half of her face, her black-rimmed glasses sitting on the bridge of her nose, and her left hand gently touching her cheek. She'd used a dramatic filter that gave her skin a soft, olive tone, and her eyes a deep blue color—an artist's choice that was not lost on Ms. Walsh.

Jennifer was a popular, pretty athlete. She was the captain of the girls' varsity soccer team and a successful student in Advanced Placement classes. Amy proceeded to show Ms. Walsh additional photos from Jennifer's social media posts. Her Instagram account was filled with images of the "perfect" teenager. Jennifer took gorgeous photos—filtered and stunning. To anyone who perused her social media, she was a dream. It was easy to see why the boys thought she was pretty, and the girls wanted to be her. But it did not sit right with Ms. Walsh.

"Amy, things aren't always what they seem."

"What do you mean?" Amy asked.

"I mean, you have no idea what it's really like to be Jennifer. Sure, these pictures tell one story, but is that really her story? When she posts pictures of her life for everyone to see, do those pictures actually reflect her life when no one is looking?"

"I don't know, does that matter?"

"Of course it matters. She, just like everyone else who posts on social media, is showing you what she wants you to see." Ms. Walsh pointed to Amy's phone.

"But she's one of the girls I've been afraid of."

"I get that, but what I am telling you is that what you see on social media is not always realistic. There's always a story, Amy. Always."

Amy's anxiety was driven by perfection, or at least what she thought was perfection. Social media exacerbated her symptoms because it shoved perfection in her face every time she signed on. It fueled her illness. What Amy, and all students with anxiety, aren't able to see is that social media is not realistic. Students with anxiety use social media and see perfection. It's a picture of what they don't think they'll ever be. If educators are advocates for students with anxiety, they must teach them how to navigate the false perfection shown in social media.

LEAD **FORWARD** STRATEGY
Be Realistic about Social Media

Social media is a filtered version of reality and results in a skewed perception of happiness and success. Users dictate what they present to their peers, showing only the best versions of themselves: their good sides. It can be difficult enough for adults to weed through the filters and remind themselves that for every supermom who succeeds at meal prep on Sunday afternoon after running a half marathon, there is also a moment of imperfection. Perhaps she yelled at her son for walking through the house with muddy shoes, forgot to bake for the PTO fundraiser, or got a coffee stain on a new white dress just before a board meeting.

But for students with anxiety, perception equals reality.

The world of communication our students now live in is almost entirely electronic and, by default, completely fabricated. Students with anxiety who are already struggling with their self-perceptions become even more self-conscious when they see that fabricated perfection. Any self-worth they might have had is depleted. Trying to "keep up with the Joneses" has become a daily reality for students with anxiety whenever they open a social media application. They can never turn off the images in their heads. When students don't feel like the peers they see, their anxiety increases. The constant consumption of perfection exacerbates feelings of inadequacy and drives up students' anxiety and depression.

In the book *What Made Maddy Run*, author Kate Fagan discusses the world of social media and its negative impact on young people.

> One of the trickiest parts of social media is recognizing that everyone is doing the same thing you're doing: presenting their best self.... While it's easy to understand intrinsically that your presence on social media is only

one small sliver of your full story, it's more difficult to apply that logic to everyone else.

Engaging in social media is a comfort, an opportunity to escape from the harsh realities of life. But for students with anxiety, it's not an escape at all. In an anxious mind, it is already difficult to distinguish irrational from rational, and when you give them the task of separating reality from idealism, their irrational brain will have a field day.

Further, preaching abstinence from social media doesn't work. As with many areas of life, telling students *not* to do it is just going to increase their curiosity—and result in a higher likelihood of engagement. Students with anxiety also want to engage in social media even more because it gives them an explanation for their self-deprecation. They cannot sit with the unknown. If they feel low self-worth, they need to know why—and social media gives them that why. We need to teach students with anxiety to have a healthy perspective about social media if we're going to teach them to protect themselves.

- **Avoid social media if you're in a bad mood.** Little good comes from being overly emotional, and it's even worse when it comes to social media. Teach all students, especially those with anxiety, that social media is a bad place to go when they're upset, angry, experiencing negative emotions, or anxious. Students who choose to engage in social media when they are not in a healthy frame of mind will find themselves reading or making posts that worsen their emotional states. They may be able to control what they post themselves, but they cannot control the content posted by others. And students with anxiety cannot control how their minds use that content against them.

  When a student is feeling anxious, give them a

different task rather than indulging their desire to log on to social media. Talk with them about what makes them feel good. Take a walk with them; play a game. Keep their mind and their hands occupied rather than letting them reach for their phones, and teach them to do that for themselves when you're not around.

- **Teach students to ask questions about what they see.** Social media presents us with snapshots of other people's lives, like data points on a graph. No one post shows the full story. Instead of coming to conclusions based on what they see on social media, students need to start asking questions within their minds. Just because Jennifer posted a picture of her smiling in front of a friend's pool, does that mean she was happy throughout the entire day? Encourage students to tap into their innate curiosity. What happened earlier in the morning, before Jennifer got to the pool? Did she get into an argument with her mother about when to be home? Did she try on multiple bathing suits before leaving, only to find that many of them no longer hugged her hips the way she'd hoped?

  A single picture can be a prompt. Encourage students to write their own stories about what they see, to give them a healthier perspective. Make social media a prompt for an assignment. Have them pick a post they saw and write an imperfect story about it. This will help them get used to the idea that perfect pictures don't tell a perfect story.

- **Encourage journaling.** Life is about balance and moderation. Educators need to teach students that when they go "all in" in one capacity, they need to counter it by going "all in" in another. Encourage students to invest as much time in themselves as they do the lives of others. Each time they choose to engage in social media, challenge them to spend an equivalent amount of time writing and reflecting on themselves. Students need a space to be authentic, especially after they've been bathed in a filtered version of reality. Ask them to journal about what they saw and how they feel. Having a place to "talk" about the pressures and anxieties they feel after looking at the "lives" of peers will help them separate reality from fantasy. This is an exercise that students with anxiety should engage in regularly. Ms. Walsh's conversation with Amy was a way of helping her process the image of Jennifer she saw on social media. Journaling is a way for them to do it on their own.

Saying No to Cell Phones

Todd had struggled with anxiety and separation since he started school as a five-year-old. He found it hardest to fight that panic when he was around his peers. His internal dialogue was always trying to convince him that he couldn't compete, that he wasn't ever going to be as good as they were. He felt safe in the classroom, in the confines of a lesson or activity, and when his mind was preoccupied with a tangible goal. But during recess or lunch, he started to feel anxious. In those moments, he judged himself against his classmates: his looks, his lunch, his clothes, his haircut, his sneakers, his school supplies, his athleticism ...

His anxiety outside of the classroom continued to get worse with each passing school year, and he started to rely on his time in the classroom to manage it. That seemed to work until he entered middle school—when everyone, including him, started getting cell phones.

Todd never imagined that a cell phone, the one item he couldn't wait to possess, would end up making his anxiety even worse. Suddenly, his one escape during the day—the classroom—lost its comfort. The quiet time when he was free of the comparisons of the playground now became a time when he pulled out his phone. He would finish his work and jump on his phone, checking Twitter, Snapchat, and Instagram. He saw images of friends hanging out, kids in new kicks, and boys celebrating winning goals—all situations he hated about the free time of lunch, gym, and recess. His anxiety began to intensify, but it wasn't until his principal took a risky position to ban cell phones in the classroom that he learned why.

When the student body heard that the school was likely to adopt a "no cell phone" policy, they tried every tactic they could to prevent it from happening, and Todd was right there with them. Students sent emails, attended forums, and even started a petition to ban the policy from taking effect.

Regardless of their efforts, though, the new policy was enacted just after spring break. Although it took time to get used to, Todd quickly found that his anxiety decreased during the school day. After about a week, he found himself feeling comfortable in class again, and focusing on the assigned work rather than beating himself up over what everybody else was up to. It became obvious that his inability to access social media during class helped him return to feeling comfortable there.

Todd's school took a smart risk in implementing a "no cell phone" policy. It helped students with anxiety, like Todd, if they were protected from social media during class time. The policy allowed them to "turn off" their anxiety, and being able to do that for any amount of time is a welcome change.

LEAD **FORWARD** STRATEGY
Eliminate Social Media from the Classroom

When students are suffering from anxiety, they aren't thinking rationally and can't determine what they need in a given moment. It might not be a popular decision, but we need to remove social media from their world, especially for students with anxiety, even if it's only for a short time.

It is easy to get sucked into any activity or mindset. I'm sure you've all been guilty of falling into a YouTube black hole. You start by looking at a video of a young child's reaction to turning on cochlear implants for the first time, only to come back to reality an hour later, wondering how and why you're watching a video of a man doing magic tricks for a monkey at the zoo.

With all the demands of life, it can be easy to succumb to uplifting and silly videos on the internet; it's an escape, a release. But it can be just as easy to fall into a black hole of videos that *don't* make you feel good about yourself. Everyone has an internal dialogue: fears, doubts, unworthiness, and unhappiness.

Teach students to practice mindfulness (the ability to focus on the present even amidst the "noise" of your inner voice) regularly. It can give anxious students a break from the doubt in their minds.

At times, that voice is stronger than usual, but for students with anxiety, that inner voice is much louder than most. It's a voice that is more easily persuaded. It tells you you're not good enough, that it's not going to turn out right, and that you're as far from perfect as they come. It's fueled by the happiness and success of others. A student like Todd sees a smiling "Snap" from a friend, an image of their girlfriend smiling at the beach, or friends getting off a ski lift, and that voice now has a script. Social media becomes a black hole of unhappiness relentlessly pulling its victim toward the deep, dark, gripping center. The only way to counteract this is by eliminating social media from the classroom in the following ways:

- **Implement a no cell phone policy.** Todd's school made a drastic, unpopular change by implementing this sort of policy. The administrative team might not have had control over their students' social media use for twenty-four hours a day, but for the seven and a half hours that they did, they decided to eliminate its impact on their school community. Within a week, students like Todd felt freedom from their anxiety, at least for a little while.

  With a zero tolerance policy on cell phones, educators reduce social media's impact on the mental health of students with anxiety. The ability to "log off" for any length of time will help the most anxious students "turn off" their inner voices. Whether it's ten minutes, fifty minutes, or seven and a half hours, any break for an anxious mind is a welcomed one.

  This strategy is simple: Advocating for students with anxiety means not allowing them access to their cell phones during class time. If your school isn't going to implement a policy, then start small. Begin by asking students to put their phones away for minutes at a time. I've seen educators ask students to place their phones on their desks so they can monitor if/when they attempt to use them. Once students can leave their phones alone for a small period of time, increase the expectation. Continue to build the time up until they find themselves surviving without their phones for the duration of the class.

  From there, make a policy that says phones can't be

out at all. Use a shoe organizer that hangs on the door as a cell phone sleeve in the classroom. Assign students a slot and have them place their phones in the organizer upon entering. Whatever strategy you use, the bottom line is simple. Anxious students are more productive when they are free from their phones, so they can't compare themselves to others.

- **Teach students to pay attention.** Unfortunately, not even the strongest no cell phone policy is airtight. Fill in those gaps by teaching students to practice mindfulness (the ability to focus on the present even amidst the "noise" of your inner voice) regularly. It can give anxious students a break from the doubt in their minds.

The mind is a muscle. Every time you put your mind to use, you are "working out." School is a long, intense workout for students' minds, five days a week for seven and a half hours a day. If students were to engage in a seven-and-a-half-hour leg set, you would tell them to take breaks. But we respond differently when it's an equally long brain set. Mindfulness is forced rest. It's a way of slowing the mind down. It doesn't mean forcing the brain not to think; it means teaching the brain to tune in to thoughts that aren't judgmental.

Practicing mindfulness just prior to an exam can decrease student anxiety and increase student performance. Stu Singer, a sports psychology consultant with WellPerformance, teaches a six-one-seven breathing technique that allows students to hear their inner thoughts, but doesn't allow them to give these thoughts any credence or judgment. Although a majority of his work is with elite athletes, his lessons and techniques apply to students as well, since academia is also a performance stage. "True success," Singer says, "is based on a foundation that can handle setbacks and challenges."

These challenges for many of your most anxious students are the filtered happiness they see on social media.

Start by practicing two minutes of mindfulness at the beginning of class. Make it part of your daily agenda. From there, start implementing it just before assessments or other big projects. Do this with the students. The goal is for mindfulness to become a student's go-to, rather than their phone.

MOVING **FORWARD**

The twenty-first-century lives our students live are supersaturated with filtered media that present a world of fabricated happiness and success. This fuels the self-doubt that your anxious students feel, and creates a world of competition that exacerbates mental illness. Educators must work to reduce the impact of social media on students with anxiety. If you can't implement "no cell phone" policies in your entire school, you must find a way around them. Teach mindfulness and/or eliminate cell phones from your classrooms.

We know that even our best efforts won't eliminate cell phones from classrooms, so we must teach students with anxiety to engage with social media in a healthy way. Encourage students not to log in if they are feeling anxious. If they engage in social media when they are angry or depressed, or experiencing anxiety, it will likely result in increased self-loathing. Teach them that most situations are not as they appear. Encourage them to ask themselves questions about the posts they see: Did anyone get into a fight with their parents that morning? How many of their friends were more worried about how they looked in the picture than they were about having a wonderful time?

You can even use a social media post as an activity prompt to engage students with anxiety in a meaningful and productive way.

And finally, make journaling a habit in your classroom. For every minute a student spends engaging in social media, have them write in a journal for one minute. Journaling gives an anxious student's inner voice the microphone without interruption. We want a student's anxiety to have a voice, so the student can then move on to a more proactive practice. Journaling not only provides an anxious student with an opportunity to address their anxiety, but it also gives them a healthier perspective on the fantasy world of perfection that they see on social media.

THINK **ABOUT** IT

1. How could you reduce the amount of time students spend on social media?

2. How often are you engaged in unproductive social media during the day, and what could you do instead?

3. If your school does not have a "no cell phone" policy, how could you go about getting one passed?

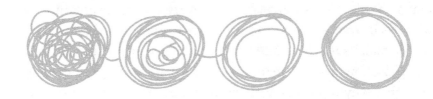

CHAPTER 6

Get Students to Buy In

Know Your Why and Effectively Communicate It to Anxious Students

The one thing that you have that nobody else has is you. Your voice, your mind, your story, your vision. So write and draw and build and play and dance and live as only you can.

— NEIL GAIMAN, BESTSELLING AUTHOR

TEACHING IS HELD to more scrutiny than many other professions. We've all been to school, so we all claim to know how best to do it. In the decades since we educators were in grade school, the content hasn't changed much. With the exception of a deeper history, math is still math, reading is still reading, and the scientific method is still, well, the scientific method.

So if content hasn't changed, why has teaching changed?

The variables educators face in the classrooms today are the students themselves. Teachers are no longer expected to stand and deliver content the way our teachers did. Instead, we have to connect to our students. We need to let them know we care about them ... while still selling our content.

This is vitally important for teachers who handle anxious students. Students with anxiety fight every day to maintain control over their worlds. If we expect them to hand us the control, we better make sure they can buy into what we are selling. Educators need to know why we are doing what we are doing, and communicate that why to our students with anxiety if we are going to connect with them and help them find success in today's classrooms.

A Student's Teacher

Cheryl was midway through her first year as an administrator in a new district. She was still learning the culture of the school and staff members, but as she worked more closely with students, she quickly began to learn the reputations in the building. Students weren't shy about which teachers they liked and which ones they didn't. Because Cheryl was new to the district, she hesitated to put much stock in what the students expressed. She evaluated many teachers, so whenever one started to get a reputation because of student complaints, she sought the advice of her administrative colleagues to get a feel for whether or not the students were exaggerating.

Surprisingly, Cheryl was finding that students were typically accurate in their assessments.

Mr. Walker was a veteran teacher in the math department. He taught mostly freshmen in both honors and college prep classes. His classroom was highly structured and so, too, were his unit plans. He expected students to come to class, sit in rows, and take notes. He assigned homework every night, and students were quizzed on their notes a few times each unit, and then given a standard assessment at the unit's end. Mr. Walker's classroom was the epitome of teacher-centered. If students weren't following the lesson, he expected them to ask questions or stay after for extra help. There was little student-centered work that would allow students to discover the curriculum or determine where they might need support. His gradebook was about as underwhelming as his unit plans: *homework 1.2, quiz 1.1, test 1.*

Cheryl was working with the freshman class and was responsible for their discipline and any necessary interventions. In the first few months, she began noticing a trend in the number of students who were cutting Mr. Walker's class. In addition, she dealt with a number of student conflicts involving Mr. Walker.

Denise was a freshman in Mr. Walker's honors geometry class. She wasn't a habitual school offender, but she was being sent to Cheryl's office more and more frequently. Cheryl hadn't realized that Denise was getting to a breaking point until the day when a school adjustment counselor called her and asked to talk about a complaint Denise had made.

Evidently, Denise was not getting along with Mr. Walker and had told her adjustment counselor that his teaching style wasn't working for her. She wasn't someone who could learn just from listening, and hated it when Mr. Walker randomly called on her. She was failing a majority of the quizzes and tests in his class and did not feel supported. Whenever she tried to approach him to ask a question, he told her that she wasn't doing well because she wasn't completing the homework. According to Denise, Mr. Walker believed her lack of success was her own fault.

> *Educators need to know why we are doing what we are doing, and communicate that why to our students with anxiety if we are going to connect with them and help them find success in today's classrooms.*

Cheryl called Mr. Walker in for a meeting with Denise, feeling that the best way to help Denise was to mediate the conflict before it got worse. She also called Denise's mother to tell her about the plan before scheduling the meeting. Denise's mother told Cheryl the same concerns about Mr. Walker that Denise had shared, and Cheryl promised to call her with a follow-up once the mediation took place.

Mr. Walker asked to meet with Cheryl fifteen minutes before the mediation. He wanted to let her know his side of the story.

"Denise does very little in class. Her homework is rarely complete, if she does it at all, and she won't ask any questions during class time."

"Perhaps she doesn't feel comfortable speaking up in front of her peers," Cheryl suggested. From her conversations with Denise's adjustment counselor, Cheryl knew Denise was suffering from anxiety and struggled with speaking up in class, even when asked.

"Well, that's no excuse. If she wants to be successful, she has to ask questions. She hasn't even come after school to see me."

"I understand that, but ..." Cheryl tried again to advocate for Denise. It was important for Mr. Walker to understand Denise's anxiety if she was going to be successful in his class. She thought that if she explained the symptoms of her anxiety now, the mediation might be more productive.

Unfortunately, Mr. Walker was too quick to interrupt for Cheryl to make her point.

"Look, I have content I need to get through. I present the material, I give them all the resources they need, and it's up to them to be successful."

Cheryl wasn't able to get a word in edgewise with Mr. Walker. He was adamant that he was doing *everything* for *all* his students, and that they were the ones who were not following through. Cheryl's approach for the mediation quickly changed from getting each party to see where they failed to help the other, to creating a plan for Denise to make up her work. Mr. Walker was not a teacher that Cheryl was going to change. He was rigid, aggressive, and stubborn. She quickly came to see what the students were talking about: Mr. Walker wasn't a student's teacher.

Students with anxiety need teachers who are willing to analyze the potential cause of a behavior or a failing grade. Educators who are willing to do so are advocates for these students. A "student's teacher" is authentic and compassionate, patient and human (see Chapter 3). Mr. Walker was exactly what a student with anxiety *didn't* need: a rigid, black-and-white teacher who expects every student to fit a certain mold. These types of educators trigger students with anxiety and send them directly onto the path of avoidance—which was where Denise found herself.

If educators are going to connect with students with anxiety, they must let students know who they are. Teachers must communicate to these students *why* they are teaching what they're teaching and allow them to take some ownership over it. Only then can they teach students what they need to know to be successful. Imagine how the anxious students in Mr. Walker's class would have felt if, instead of only knowing that they had to read and take notes, they knew why Mr. Walker wanted them to be successful. Imagine if he took the time to explain why he was teaching what he was teaching—and why he was so passionate about them learning it.

Imagine if he gave them the building blocks they needed to buy in, rather than just brushing past their need to be a part of the conversation.

The bottom line was that Denise, and now Cheryl, couldn't see *why* Mr. Walker wanted to teach his students. Did he want to help all students, including the anxious ones … or did he simply want to tell them what to do and have them comply?

LEAD **FORWARD** STRATEGY
Know Why You Teach

Educators need to do all they can to build trust and connect with students who have anxiety. Being an educator is similar to being in sales, where the goal is to get the consumer to buy the product or service. The consumer can get the product anywhere, so why should they buy it from one particular salesperson? What makes the product irresistible, so the consumer believes in it and needs it? The answer is often … the person selling it. Consumers aren't buying a product or service; they're buying the salesperson and their story. Are they relatable? Believable? Trustworthy? If the consumer can answer yes to each of these questions, then they are more likely to buy from *that* salesperson.

In education, the consumers are the students and their parents. Sure, they are not "buying" a product from the teachers, but teachers are "selling" them the lessons. If the teacher is relatable, believable, and trustworthy, the student is more likely to learn from that teacher, i.e., "buy" their product. These characteristics are not born from *what* a teacher is doing or *how* they are doing it. They are born from *why* they are doing it.

All students have a better chance of succeeding when their teachers articulate the *why*, but this is even more true for students with anxiety. Too often, educators encounter students experiencing the symptoms of mental illness, and immediately resort to *how* they can help the student. But instead of asking how you can help a student suffering from anxiety, instead ask *why* you need to help them. Why do you feel the need to see that student achieve success? No matter what your why is, the passion affixed to the answer will permeate your interaction and translate to the student.

Follow these strategies to help you and your students know why you teach.

- **Show authenticity.** Be authentic, and your students will see your imperfection in all areas of life, including in your presentations, speeches, and preparedness, just to name a few. In a digital world where students are inundated with images of perfection, they must understand that such an existence only appears in the filtered, edited, uber-controlled platform that is the internet (see Chapter 5). Spending so much time in a world doctored to represent happiness and success through an unflawed lens allows students with anxiety to lose sight of reality and authenticity. Our job is to balance that increasing anxiety. Educators who are authentic and imperfect give that balance.

  Start the year with a project about why you're all there. Participate with your students. Let them get to know who you are. Share the ups and downs, a funny story or two. Make yourself less of a "scary" authority figure in the room, and you will communicate to students with anxiety that you do not expect perfection.

- **Have conversations.** When educators know their why, they open up to healthy, necessary conversations with students. Students with anxiety need educators to give them that chance to express what they are feeling. Start with eliminating classic homework checks. Rather than going around the room and spot-checking student work, group students and get them talking about the work. While this is going on, visit each group and talk with the students about their evening, when they did their work or why they couldn't, and impress upon them that the idea is to perfect the skill, not necessarily to have done so on their own the night before. Making homework conversations the norm will make talking feel more natural for students with anxiety, and help you communicate to them that imperfection is normal.

• **Trust your students.** Building trust is at the core of every positive relationship an educator has with a student. When educators are driven by a why, they are more likely to be cerebral, to listen, and to ask questions. All of these are necessary for students with anxiety, who are often emotional and finalistic. If they can trust you, they'll buy into you as more than just an educator, but as a mentor too. When you engage in conversations with your students, keep your mind free from drafted, ready-to-go responses. *If Johnny says this, I'm still going to tell him it's a zero.* Ask the question and listen, trusting them to tell you what you need to know. Ask what you need to know to clarify the situation, and then respond. Trust that the students are telling you the truth, for those who are anxious will be more likely to see you as an advocate and less as a barrier or trigger.

Miscommunication

Ms. Violet was a veteran teacher with an unfavorable reputation. She was seen as an aggressive, opinionated loudmouth. One wonders how she became a teacher in the first place, and the explanation was simple: she wasn't completely ineffective.

Ms. Violet was divisive. She had a camp of colleagues and students who loved her, and a camp who did not. If everyone could agree on one thing, it was that she got the kids' attention. Whether it was in the classroom, the cafeteria, or at graduation, she always found a way to make herself heard. In the classroom, she was unpredictable. She'd throw books across the room for dramatic effect, or tell the students they were being pathetic. In the cafeteria, she'd yell at students to sit down and be quiet, and her short stature was a sight to see when coupled with her loud antics. At graduation, the beach ball being tossed about by the eager graduates during ceremonial speeches always seemed to find its way to her, the scrooge who stalked off with everybody's source of fun.

But all the shenanigans aside, some students liked Ms. Violet. They found her intelligent, smart, and devoted. They never doubted where her heart was, or her selflessness when it came to helping students in need. But the students who felt this way were few and far between. It wasn't that this view of Ms. Violet was wrong or even unfair; in fact, it was quite accurate. But Ms. Violet never found a way to let her motivations outshine her behaviors.

Students with anxiety saw her differently. For them, her reputation was a true account of who she was: mean, aggressive, and unreasonable. Many students who struggled with anxiety even described her as a bully. They couldn't see why she bothered to teach in the first place. Why would anyone so grumpy, so negatively impacted by the presence of children, work in a school? Her presence alone would trigger anxious students.

All those who either liked Ms. Violet or worked with her (working with her didn't mean you had to like her), though, knew she was passionate about young people and their future success. She worked long, hard hours to find better ways to reach them, and created courses that were effective, stimulating, and worthwhile. Where she failed was in her ability to communicate this to *all* her students. Students with anxiety never were able to get on board with her methods because they didn't understand why she did what she did. Ms. Violet represented lost potential for students with anxiety: she had all the passion those students needed, but none of the savvy to communicate it effectively. Instead of being seen as the dedicated, driven educator, Ms. Violet was feared, avoided, and even loathed by students with even the slightest anxiety.

Ms. Violet knew her why, but didn't know how to communicate it to her students. Instead of helping them, she made her anxious ones more anxious.

LEAD **FORWARD** STRATEGY
Communicate the Why

Anxiety is calmed in a trusting, predictable, and overt environment, so educators must do more than know their why. Students with anxiety need educators who can effectively communicate their why through behavior and actions. Do that, and your most anxious students will buy into your teaching and succeed in your classroom.

Every day, young minds curious to know "why" sit in front of educators across the world. *Why do we have to do homework? Why are we writing an essay instead of doing a project? Why do you only let us write in blue or black pen? Why was Kennedy assassinated? Why do you want to help me?* No matter how important or relevant the topic in question is, students need *and want* to know why. *Why is Mrs. Ravesi-Weinstein a teacher? Why does Mr. Walker just lecture? Why am I feeling this way?*

Not all questions are verbalized. Most of the time, the most important questions remain unasked. Instead, students sit with their "whys" and come up with their own answers. Welcome to one of the favorite pastimes of an anxious mind. Students with anxiety ask *why* and *what if* all the time.

"Why do I have to take math? What if I don't understand it?"

"Why can't I live in the city? What if I have a panic attack on the train?"

"Why does Mr. Walker always assign papers? What if I can't express myself in written form?"

Students with anxiety always challenge themselves to know why, whether openly or in silence. Educators must be aware of this and be proactive. Rather than being at odds with anxious students about why—both yours and theirs—and running the risk of making them school- or work-avoidant, tell them why. Have a conversation with them. Do them a favor and save them the energy by answering the question for them. This will take their minds off extraneous material and get them to buy into your methods. They'll find success in the classroom. Here are ways to communicate your why for anxious students:

- **Ask students what they think.** We all bring preconceived notions to the table, whether we are students or educators. When we ask a question, we may not know the answer, but we likely have thoughts as to what the answer might be. Tap into this potential whenever a student asks, "Why?" Instead of responding with your answer, ask them, "What do you think?" with equal curiosity. Use a supportive, friendly tone to move you closer to authenticity, conversation, and trust. Always validate the thoughts of a student with anxiety. Tell them "good thinking," or "I hadn't thought of that," even if they aren't correct. The two most important results of a conversation like this are that students walk away knowing why, as well as why they didn't have all the information before. (To learn more about how to create a culture of inquiry in your classroom, see Connie Hamilton's book *Hacking Questions*, also by Times 10.)

- **Be transparent.** Although transparency is essential for *all* students, it's essential for students with anxiety. They are the least likely to ask why, but they certainly want—and need—to know. Understand that the question is there and that you're going to make an impact by answering it. Jon Saphier, the founder and president of Research for Better Teaching, is known for his concept of "No Secrets Teaching." When we have a "no secrets" classroom, Saphier explains, "our underperforming students quickly conclude that the extra effort we exert to make sure they understand objectives and criteria for success represents our genuine desire for them to succeed and our belief in their ability to do so."

This concept holds true for anxious students when we communicate our why. They start to understand why we teach, why we want to help them, and why they can be successful in our classrooms. Let your why drive your actions in your classroom, including all your asks. If your objective is the why of a lesson, your why is the objective of the class. Remind students daily why you do what you do, whether through actions or words, and they'll start to learn that they can trust you.

- **Participate in the class.** Many teachers choose to spend time on the first few days of school breaking the ice with students. We need to get to know the students, and the students need to get to know each other. Too often, teachers facilitate these activities but aren't active participants. You are part of the classroom community, too, and arguably the most important part. Break the ice with your students. Let them learn about you and your why. An effective speaker wouldn't engage with the audience before introducing themselves and building a connection with them. It should be the same in classrooms. Tell your students who you are and why you teach. Remind them of why you teach whenever you can. Perhaps it becomes your class theme. If you see it as worth doing, then anxious students will too.

MOVING **FORWARD**

Why do you teach? Why do you show up every day? What keeps you planning lessons and delivering instruction? What is *your* why? If *you* know and communicate your why, your *students* can know your why.

Students with anxiety easily get overwhelmed. All the "whats" in their world can become crippling. But if you redirect students to the why of each task via examples of our own whys, you can get them to see that each job is just one small, attainable goal in the journey of learning (see Chapter 2).

Knowing your why makes you authentic, trustworthy, and communicative with your students. The way you express your why should include making students a part of the discovery and being transparent by engaging in icebreakers and team-building activities *with* your classes. The most challenging part of this process is coming to know and understand your own why. Your why should be simple, straightforward, and memorable, and communicate an important truth to your students. We all have a story that explains how we ended up in education, but *why* are you still here? This is what your students with anxiety need to explicitly know if they are going to trust you and give you control.

THINK **ABOUT** IT

1. As an educator, what is your why?

2. How can you communicate your why to your students productively and consistently?

3. How can you encourage students to communicate their own whys, and why is this important?

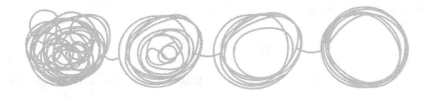

CHAPTER 7

Give Students a Voice

Encourage Self-Expression and Self-Advocacy as a Way to Manage Anxiety

But you are not alone in this.
— "Timshel" by Mumford and Sons, rock band

ANXIETY IS A game of control. It exists in students who have a desperate need to control situations. When they feel out of control, anxiety festers and shows them all the ways in which a situation could go wrong. The symptoms of anxiety run the gamut and depend on the individual. From shortness of breath to upset stomach to tears, anxiety can be brutal.

As hard as it is to experience anxiety, it can be just as difficult to watch someone suffering from it. You instinctively want to take the symptoms away to make the person feel better and back in control of their emotions. But stepping in and managing the solution often does more harm than good. It might solve the anxiety in the moment, but it doesn't give the sufferer control for their next inevitable battle with anxiety. Rather than separating the student from the trigger, educators must help them find their voice as a way of managing their anxiety. Doing this requires encouraging self-advocacy and self-expression.

Overstepping

Every day, Mrs. Rutland, assistant principal, would check her calendar to plan out her day. Typically, she had standing administrative meetings, student intervention support teams with adjustment and guidance counselors, and lunch duty. The variables of her days were in the parent meetings, IEP team meetings, and discipline hearings scheduled by her administrative assistant.

On this particular day, when looking at her calendar, she saw that she was scheduled to meet with Andrea and her mom, Tina, about a potential 504 plan. Andrea had recently been diagnosed with chronic anxiety. School staff were working to learn the specifics and collaborating with her mom on appropriate support. Although Mrs. Rutland was grateful to have a parent so invested in her child's schooling, she struggled with the intensity of her interactions with Tina. Mrs. Rutland found that they spent less time talking about Andrea's needs and more time talking about Tina's requests.

Mrs. Rutland arrived at the meeting and was not surprised to see Andrea's guidance counselor, Ms. Michaelson, in attendance. Ms. Michaelson was responsible for drafting the 504 plan. One attendee Mrs. Rutland was surprised to see, however, was the principal, Mr. Johnson. Thus far, Mrs. Rutland had led all of the meetings. She assumed Tina had emailed Mr. Johnson directly, or that Ms. Michaelson reached out to him for assistance.

"Thank you, everyone, for coming to this meeting," began Mr. Johnson. "I know I haven't been directly involved in Andrea's case, but Tina asked if I could be going forward. I know that Ms. Michaelson and Mrs. Rutland have been working to assist Andrea as she navigates her new diagnosis. Today, you asked to reconvene the team and have me present to deal with Andrea's concerns related to her math class, is that correct?"

"Yeah, that is exactly right," said Tina. "Andrea has missed many classes because she just doesn't feel like she can work with Mrs. Cutler. She feels Mrs. Cutler doesn't like her, and Andrea is struggling with her teaching style. She makes Andrea feel panicky and anxious. I know we have drafted language for a 504 plan, but I don't think those accommodations are going to address her math class right now, which is her biggest trigger."

"Ms. Michaelson, have you addressed math previously?" Mr. Johnson asked.

"We have," Ms. Michaelson answered. "When Tina first brought up concerns about math in an email to Mrs. Cutler, we had a conference call to address the specific concerns. Andrea felt like Mrs. Cutler was not accommodating or understanding enough of her anxiety. She felt like Mrs. Cutler called her out in class for not completing a makeup test on time."

"Did you feel the conflict was resolved?" Mr. Johnson asked Andrea.

Tina chimed in instead. "The conversation went well and I felt like Ms. Michaelson did a great job mediating. However, Andrea still does not feel comfortable going to Mrs. Cutler for help. It's simple: Mrs. Cutler triggers Andrea's anxiety. I am asking that the 504 reflect that Andrea can be taken out of her math class."

The looks around the table were aghast. At least Tina was cutting to the point, but it was a bold request, and one that they usually did not draft into a 504 plan.

"I understand your concerns about math," agreed Mr. Johnson. "However, we cannot put that request into Andrea's 504 plan. Additionally, we can't just remove a student from a class without making sure we've exhausted all other avenues first."

"We have," stated Tina.

"Has she tried staying for extra help with Mrs. Cutler? Has a plan to complete makeup work been put into place?" asked Mr. Johnson.

"I've told you, Andrea cannot work with Mrs. Cutler anymore. She needs to be taken out of the class." Tina was getting impatient.

"We can't just remove a student from a class without indicating it on the transcript. We also need another class for the student to enroll in. If this is what you and Andrea want, then we'll discuss the next steps associated with a decision of this nature," explained Mr. Johnson. "We will have to withdraw Andrea from the class. This means that a 'W' will appear on her transcript. We either give withdraw-fails or withdraw-medicals. In this case, given Andrea's clinical anxiety, she would be eligible for a withdraw-medical. From there, we'll look for another math class for her."

"I'm fine with the withdraw-medical. As for the new math class, we were hoping Andrea could just take a study hall and not another math class."

Mrs. Rutland was not surprised that the conversation had arrived here, but she was surprised at how blunt Tina was being.

"Giving her a study hall will not impact her this year, but it will set her back with math as she tries to complete her graduation requirements," Mr. Johnson explained. "She will need to double up in math either next year or senior year."

"Can she take a college math class in the summer and get credit for it?"

"She can, however, I wouldn't recommend it. Not having core math classes from high school will be a red flag for the more competitive colleges, in which I know Andrea is interested."

"I don't agree," indicated Tina.

"Let's hold off on that right now. We can revisit it next month as we start to build the schedule for next year." Mr. Johnson turned to face Ms. Michaelson to give her the directive. "Ms. Michaelson, can you change Andrea's schedule and reach out to Mrs. Cutler to let her know that Andrea will no longer be in her class? Mrs. Rutland, you are the point person for Tina going forward, once she decides about the math courses for junior and senior year."

And with that, Mr. Johnson ended the meeting. Mrs. Rutland and Ms. Michaelson proceeded to complete the action items assigned to them by Mr. Johnson and see to it that Andrea's anxiety about math was resolved.

Not surprisingly, the change in Andrea's schedule did not eliminate anxiety from her life. Removing a trigger doesn't remove the illness; it simply allows it to fester elsewhere in the student's life.

Tina was trying to be a supportive mother. She was attending school meetings and advocating for her daughter. However, as I often see with the families of students with anxiety, she was so desperate to help her daughter that she was trying to solve her problems rather than guide her through them.

Educators need to insist that students with anxiety advocate for themselves. They need to help the students re-establish control in their lives, so they learn how to manage their anxiety. Let them drive the meetings and decisions. The request to remove Andrea from Mrs. Cutler's math class might have remained, but it would have had more impact on the student's individual fight with anxiety if it came from Andrea herself.

LEAD **FORWARD** STRATEGY
Encourage Self-Advocacy

Managing anxiety isn't about what's being asked; it's about who's asking. Educators must implement strategies to help students with anxiety become their own advocates.

An anxiety diagnosis can be overwhelming for any family. As a mother, I know how impossibly difficult it is to see your child struggling. You want to take away what is hurting them. You'd even be willing to bear the burden yourself. Imagine how hard it is as a parent to manage an invisible struggle for your child, because anxiety is exactly that: invisible. It's a constant struggle without a consistent cause. When someone is afraid of a snake, the solution is simple: take away the snake. But when your child is afraid of the unknown, parents' first instincts are to take away any possible trigger: participation in a sport or activity, a particular class that poses a challenge, or a friendship.

As understandable as this reaction is, it's one that educators must advise against for parents. Instead, work to teach students the necessary skills and give them adequate support to discover their triggers. Removing the trigger won't help students with anxiety cope, because it only removes the trigger—not the anxiety. Only students can work to combat that anxiety—and they can only do it by advocating for themselves. Teach them how to be self-advocates, so that in a meeting like the one with Tina and Andrea, Andrea would talk for herself, rather than her mother talking for her. Here are ways to get started:

- **Be available.** Being available for your students does not mean just being physically available; it means being emotionally available too. If students feel like their teachers are emotionally available, they will trust their teachers to understand them instead of judging them.

   That fear of judgment will make them far less likely to advocate for themselves—or even go to the teacher to share their thoughts.

   Being emotionally available doesn't mean you have to get personal with students and share all your feelings and thoughts. It's simpler than that. It means that you, the educator, understand that life sometimes gets in the way. Of course, life would be easier if all students simply followed the rules and policies, but that can't always happen. Perhaps Mrs. Cutler and Andrea could have avoided the initial upset if Mrs. Cutler was willing to work with Andrea to make up the test in question. Rather than penalizing Andrea for not making up the exam within the expected timeline spelled out in her classroom policies, Mrs. Cutler could have worked with Andrea's limitations.

In short, she could have made herself open and available, so that Andrea was comfortable approaching her and asking for a solution. Instead, she was closed off—and this triggered Andrea's anxiety.

The more available educators are for their students with anxiety, the more likely they are to take the risk, open up, and advocate for their own needs. Use policies as guidelines, not as the Bible, with your anxious students. Ask them what works, given their anxiety. Instead of dictating expectations, explain why they exist. Always lead with your desire for a student with anxiety to succeed. Instead of failing them because they can't make up a test within the window spelled out in your policies, ask them how you can make it work, and what will keep their anxiety from ruling the day.

- **Institute choice work.** The older we get, the more drains there are on our time. Whether it's filing taxes, food shopping, or preparing for the holidays, adulthood is the management of more and more responsibilities. One of the most important skills we learn is time management. Pass this on to your students with anxiety by continually pushing them to learn how to prioritize their time. Rather than giving them nightly homework, consider assigning all students homework two to three days in advance, and giving them opportunities during the day for choice work.

Choice work is a time in which you expect students to be engaged in independent work of their choosing. It can include working on an assignment with an approaching due date, or engaging in other activities such as coloring, video lab, reading, and activity books. Implementing choice work gives students with anxiety independence and an opportunity, with guidance and support, to begin the lifelong journey of prioritizing their time—one of the most fundamental ways to advocate for yourself. Making a schedule and sticking to it allows students with anxiety to take back control of their worlds.

Start this process by implementing choice time during your class. Ask all students to make a list of what they need to do and by when. Have them prioritize the list by assigning a 1 to the most pressing work, then a 2, 3, and so on. Once they have a picture of what must happen, have them devote the rest of their choice time to working on the most important task. Let them know that engaging in non-academic activities can be just as important as schoolwork. This is especially true for students with anxiety, who are less likely to give themselves a break—although breaks are necessary if they're to keep from burning out.

- **Hold conferences with students.** Conferences aren't just for parents anymore. I believe the most effective parent/teacher conferences happen when the teacher has already talked at length with the student. Taking time to talk with students one on one is time well spent. Use the time to provide valuable feedback to students on their academic work and set the stage to hear about their struggles. Use it to get to know students by engaging in relevant, non-academic conversations.

Your students with anxiety will benefit most from this time. It will give them a sense of control and teach them that it is okay to advocate for themselves and express their feelings. Educators often feel like they need more time to meet the basic requirements of their jobs, and might believe it's impossible to find time to meet one on one with every student consistently. However, if you build in daily choice work, you'll also build time for these meetings. Helping anxious students choose productive and beneficial choice activities is the beginning of a student conference. Take it a step further and ask the students why they are choosing to do that particular work, and you will empower the students with anxiety to speak up and be self-advocates.

Managing Fifty-Six Personalities

Charlotte and Andrew had spent the summer writing the curriculum for a new elective: the Politics of Science. The course, a co-taught science and social studies elective, was born after a cross-country trip that included four nights camping in Yellowstone National Park, the caldera of a supervolcano that experts claim is "overdue" for an eruption.

While camping, Charlotte and Andrew began thinking about whether or not the government was prepared should Yellowstone erupt. They knew that if it happened during their visit, they had no chance, but they wondered if there was an evacuation procedure in place for such a catastrophe. This was one of the questions at the core of their curriculum for the Politics of Science: Are politics and policy reflective of the scientific knowledge that we have? In other words, are lawmakers using scientific knowledge responsibly?

North Anderson High School had accepted Charlotte and Andrew's course proposal at the end of the previous school year. They were now responsible for designing a curriculum that brought their vision to reality. One of the biggest draws of the course was that students would get to choose whether or not they wanted the class to count for science credits or social studies credits. For students who did not like, or succeed, in science, it was an opportunity to get science credits for a class geared toward social studies.

Charlotte and Andrew each considered themselves curious about the other's content, but not good enough to teach it. They were looking forward to being learners in the classroom, along with their students. Additionally, it was an opportunity to see a colleague teach on a regular basis—one of the best and most effective forms of professional development any teacher can experience. They were both excited to begin what they hoped would be one of the most popular courses offered at the school.

Of course, it wasn't a perfect scenario. Administration did not see the Politics of Science as a class in which the science teacher would be grading all the science assignments, and the social studies teacher would be grading all the social studies assignments. Administration viewed the teachers' workload as an even split, regardless of the assignment's content. So while the average class size at North Anderson High was twenty-eight students, administration doubled the class size of the elective. Charlotte and Andrew showed up on the first day to a class of fifty-six eager minds awaiting their instruction. It was daunting.

The two co-teachers had already started preparing, having had the gut feeling that they would end up with a large class. So they had already begun thinking about what they could do to make a large class feel more intimate. They began planning each lesson as a series of small-group activities. Doing activities for all fifty-six students was going to be too much for students who *weren't* suffering from anxiety. Charlotte, who suffered from anxiety herself, knew that anxious students wouldn't stand a chance in the class.

Together, they implemented four corner discussions, where they would give a prompt to the class, and students would select which corner best represented their thoughts on the statement: disagree, strongly disagree, agree, strongly agree. Once they chose, they would engage with peers of similar opinions and then with those of differing opinions. While students spoke, Charlotte and Andrew filtered through the room, engaging with students, often playing devil's advocate to further fuel conversations when necessary. That way, they provided support for students with anxiety when it came to sharing their opinions. Charlotte and Andrew didn't expect those students to stand alone in any corner or speak in front of fifty-five peers about why they felt the way they did.

> **Educators must find ways to reduce the "emotional" size of the classroom so that students with anxiety can find their voices and speak up for themselves.**

Another strategy the co-teachers used was dividing a lesson into three sub-lessons. They rotated the class through the sub-lessons, sometimes taking two or more days to do so. For the lesson that focused on the spread of disease, they broke into sub-lessons. These included viewing a segment of the documentary *Death on a Factory Farm*, reading a piece from *The Jungle* by Upton Sinclair, and writing a proposal with supporting evidence, highlighting actions that individuals could take to decrease the spread of disease. Charlotte and Andrew filtered through each of the sub-lessons to support student learning, facilitate discussion, and answer questions. This created a more familiar environment for students with anxiety because it broke the larger class into groups of eighteen. It is much easier for a student with anxiety to find their voice among seventeen others than it is among fifty-five.

Following a divided lesson on renewable energy, Charlotte and Andrew received multiple emails from parents expressing how much the class was impacting their children. The lesson required students to filter through the following sub-lessons: 1. Learning how to read and analyze an electric bill, 2. Presenting a business proposal for one of eight potential energy sources, and 3. Watching a documentary on Chernobyl. The most impactful emails they received were from the parents of students who had anxiety.

> John came home from school last night and was asking me for our electric bill. He said he wanted to look at how much energy we were using and how much we were paying. In all the years I've paid utilities, I've never sat down to look at the bills this closely. When I asked John why he wanted to see the bill, he said, "We learned all about it in the Politics of Science." I've never heard him so excited about a class before. Typically, his anxiety has him just fighting to get through classes. It's not to say he doesn't like any class, but for him to be so free from his anxiety that he is excited to come home and revisit what he learned is a testament to you.

> I want to take a moment to thank you for all you do. The Politics of Science is Julia's favorite class. She talks about it every night and even asked to see the electric bill! You are doing some really cool things in class and I want to let you know that for Julia, who has anxiety, you have made her feel comfortable. Thank you again! And now to find ways to reduce my electricity!

Charlotte and Andrew were concerned about the students finding their voices in a classroom of fifty-six. This concern, although for all students, is of even greater importance for those who suffer from anxiety. It was important for Charlotte and Andrew to "decrease" the size of the classroom for everyone, but it was of utmost importance for their students with anxiety.

LEAD **FORWARD** STRATEGY
Make the Classroom Feel Smaller

Many educators find themselves with class sizes that are overwhelming and often unmanageable. Students with anxiety need their teachers to actively find solutions to this problem. Educators must find ways to reduce the "emotional" size of the classroom so that students with anxiety can find their voices and speak up for themselves.

It can take years for even the most mentally healthy individuals to acquire the skill of self-advocacy. It requires a willingness to speak up for yourself, even in difficult circumstances. Most of us find it easier to put ourselves last. As a mother, I will speak up for either of my children, but when it comes to myself, I'd rather save the energy. The larger the audience or the bigger the stage, the less comfortable self-advocacy can be. However, the safer someone feels, the more likely they are to speak up.

For students with anxiety, school can feel like standing on a cliff, exposed, with hundreds of people around, yet nobody standing by your side. Students with anxiety need help, but they know the second they call out to someone, everyone is going to turn around and see them standing there, silent and awkward. How can someone feel so alone and so on display at the same time? It's an oxymoron of sorts, but no matter how counterintuitive it may be, it is the classroom experience for many anxious students.

One of the essential strategies an educator can implement to benefit students with anxiety is to make the world that's rushing by seem smaller and less overwhelming. Charlotte and Andrew were able to succeed in doing this in a room with fifty-six students. Adopt these strategies to achieve this in your classroom.

- **Be a facilitator.** By looking at their roles less as teachers and more as facilitators, Charlotte and Andrew were able to make the classroom feel smaller for their students. They planned activities that always included discussion as a means of getting student opinions to drive the class. Teaching can no longer just be the *delivery* of information or skills. Instead, it must be a matter of organizing time to get students to *discover* information or skills. Design lessons to get students engaged in thoughtful discourse with others—both adults and classmates. When you provide students with anxiety with the opportunity to engage, they feel valued. They no longer feel like a number sitting in a room, suffering from anxiety. They feel like a human being with valuable contributions.

  In fact, Charlotte and Andrew's final exam simply facilitated an opportunity for students to explain what they learned, when they learned it, and who among them in the room influenced their change in thinking. Providing students with anxiety a safe place to contribute makes fifty-six feel more like ten.

  Start by getting students to talk to one or two classmates. From there, increase the size of the groups. The idea is to get your students with anxiety slowly accustomed to sharing their thoughts and opinions with their classmates. You can also ask students to share their thoughts in writing, but make sure to reply to their writing. This way, you are validating their opinions and showing students with anxiety that even though they have shared their thoughts, they are still in control.

The Politics of Science
Final Exam

1. **Just because we can, should we?** Using three well-developed examples from class as your evidence, take a yes or no position. You may not take an intermediate position.

2. **How has this class challenged your prior beliefs?** Taking one issue we discussed in class, explain your position on the issue before, discuss what it was we did in class that changed your opinion and finally, tell us what your beliefs about the issue are now.

Image 7.1: This shows the simple yet effective final exam from The Politics of Science class.

- **Design sub-lessons.** Charlotte and Andrew rarely delivered instruction to all fifty-six students at once. They designed sub-lessons to get students engaged in various activities that supported the growth and development of one idea. Whether it was the spread of disease, energy, or even warfare, the students in the Politics of Science class were reading, watching, collaborating, and debating on topics in a circuit of lessons. By designing and implementing sub-lessons, you can split the class size in half, thirds, or fourths, depending on the number of sub-lessons. Social and emotional health aside, mathematically, eighteen to nineteen students in a "class" is much less overwhelming than fifty-six, or even twenty-eight.

Your students with anxiety will do better in this environment. They will get more out of each lesson, because rather than using their energy to fight the anxiety they feel in a large group, they are comfortable and focusing on the lesson. Start by designing your lessons backward. Think about where you want the students to end up, and then determine the information they need to acquire along the way. Each piece of information can be acquired independently as a sub-lesson. Figure out what each sub-lesson will include and rotate groups of students through them. This is another way of implementing checkpoints in your lessons. Doing one task at a time works well for students with anxiety, who will feel more in control—and more likely to share their voices.

- **Prioritize student collaboration.** One of our natural tendencies when we get overwhelmed is to recoil and enter survival mode—fight or flight. Students with anxiety want to be invisible. They'll either find a way to leave the classroom (typically through misbehaving), or they'll sit and be quiet and unassuming. When it comes to self-advocacy and making the classroom feel smaller, these options aren't going to cut it. Instead, educators must rely on a collaborative learning environment where students are asked to speak in front of six students rather than fifty-six. A smaller group makes students with anxiety feel invested and valued, rather than overwhelmed.

  Look at a lesson plan and envision it as a student-centered collaboration. Instead of disseminating information, divide the material into categories and ask groups of students to research topics and share the information with their classmates. This will feel less intimidating to students with anxiety. Their minds will be busy working with less material and fewer people. They will feel less isolated and better able to find their voice.

Creativity Is Voice

Michael was struggling to stay in school. He was an English Language Learner who was running out of time; he would soon "age out" of the district. He was truant nine days out of ten and was dealing with significant anxiety that began after experiencing a traumatic event as a preteen in his native country of Brazil. Upon arriving in the United States and enrolling in William Exeter High School, Michael's anxiety became a significant roadblock to his academic success. Initially, his struggles began in the classroom. Being an EL level 1 student made comprehending material and completing work in classes other than his ELD course difficult and trying. Adding academic hardship to his already reeling emotional life, Michael started skipping more and more school. By the time I met him, he was a nineteen-year-old junior poised to repeat the eleventh grade. The chances of Michael becoming a dropout were high.

The first time I met Michael, we were waiting for his mother to arrive so we could conduct a meeting about his future options outside of high school. I was sitting with him and his guidance counselor, who was present to interpret for both him and his mother. It was obvious that Michael and his counselor had established a rapport. Michael was quiet and shy, but it was immediately apparent that he was a highly likable young man.

"Michael, show Mrs. Weinstein your art," said the counselor.

I looked quizzically at Michael, wondering what the counselor was talking about. Michael became shy and dropped his head in his lap, where his seemingly empty backpack sat. Reluctantly, he opened his bag and began searching for the art his counselor mentioned. He pulled out a roll of wire, wire cutters, and then a sculpture of a dinosaur.

My eyes widened and my jaw dropped. There in front of me was a gorgeous wire sculpture that looked exactly like a dinosaur.

"Michael makes these amazing wire sculptures as a hobby," explained the counselor. "He does incredible work." Then she turned to Michael and asked, "Where do you get the materials again?"

"I just find the wire lying around work, unused," Michael explained in broken English.

"And you just shape it into whatever you think of?" the counselor asked.

"Yeah," Michael responded coyly.

"It's awesome," I said admiringly. "I've never seen art like that. You're very talented."

Michael quickly put his sculpture and materials back into his bag. My heart broke for him as he hid his talent once more and sat ready to face a reality that, for him, was another trigger in a world that was already too overwhelming for his mental health. If only the school could support his hobby and happiness, maybe he would have been a graduate rather than a dropout less than one year later.

Educators must embrace the comforts found by students with anxiety. Not all students with anxiety will find successful coping strategies in the world of academia. Perhaps they will find ways to manage their anxiety in traditional classrooms the more educators understand how to help them. If a student with anxiety does have an outlet for their anxiety, we must embrace it and find a way to incorporate it into their daily routines. Michael was an artist, even if he didn't paint or draw. He should have received time and credits for his craft. But because the high school didn't have a place for him to work with wire, he never had an activity to look forward to—a time during the school day in which he would win over his anxiety.

We need to allow anxious students to be creative in school. Creativity is the ultimate form of self-expression and voice. For students with anxiety, schools need to allow and give credit for these outlets.

LEAD **FORWARD** STRATEGY
Incorporate Creativity into the Classroom

School obviously includes a highly intensive academic component. After all, one purpose of schooling is to prepare students for post-secondary schooling. But with the highly intense world of academia comes challenges and responsibilities that exacerbate already existing mental health issues. Often, anxiety is an illness that centers around control, and since students don't have control over assignments or tests, school itself can be a trigger. Rather than wasting energy fighting that, we can find a way around it. If anxious students can find outlets through creativity, we can take advantage of that and let them use those outlets.

- **Design creativity corners.** Creativity corners allow students time to engage in personal coping strategies. Creativity can be uncomplicated. Michael was a talented artist, but creativity isn't always sophisticated. Students simply need to have time to explore the corners of their minds that aren't so controlled/regulated by due dates and assignments.

  I am an educator engaged in high-stakes, intense work with many due dates. But one of the ways I keep from burning out is by taking time every day to be creative without expectations. I color, make videos of myself doing everyday activities and add music to make it funny, and work out three to five times a week—an activity that requires me to be creative to keep it interesting.

Creativity keeps us going. Michael felt good about his art, but he had to do it outside of school since there was no place for wire sculpting in the course catalog. Sure, the high school had art classes, but none of them allowed for the art in which Michael wanted to engage.

If schools had creativity corners, similar to the idea of a makerspace, maybe Michael would have been able to better cope with his anxiety. Maybe he would have had a reason to stay in school.

Self-advocacy can be nonverbal. Creative outlets are one of the best ways for students with anxiety to advocate for themselves and their own needs. Survey your students to find out what they do to express themselves. Once you have a list of the various activities, highlight one of them every week and offer time during the week to allow students to either engage in their activity or share it with a classmate. This is an excellent use of choice work time. For students with anxiety, just answering the survey is a way of advocating for themselves, and they will appreciate the opportunity to do so. If you can then incorporate time into your class for them to engage in that activity, they will feel empowered to advocate for themselves more often.

- **Make positivity notebooks.** The world in which we live is full of feedback and opinions. Daily, we are inundated with the thoughts and opinions of others. They can be specific to us and the work we do, or benign and not worth our time. But regardless of how much noise others make, one fact is always true: no matter how many positives we hear—compliments on our clothing, emails thanking us for all our hard work, or notes of appreciation—the negative feedback is always the loudest. If twenty-five staff members thank you for your hard work on designing and implementing an alternative schedule for the first two days of school, it's the one request from your boss to stay off your phone during meetings that is going to have the greatest impact.

In the book *Hacking School Discipline* by Times 10, authors Nathan Maynard and Brad Weinstein talk about the brain's natural wiring for negativity and how it impacts student behavior: "The human brain is wired to pay more attention to the negative than the positive. Awareness of this bias and a focused effort to override it can create more optimistic students who are less stressed and more likely to respond than react." Maynard and Weinstein suggest educators "delve into moments of positivity."

No matter how rarely a student with anxiety hears negative comments, the weight of those comments will smother all of the positive ones people have said to them, and this inevitably fuels self-doubt.

Encourage students with anxiety to keep a notebook of all the positive activities that have happened. Whether they're text messages, Tweets, Snaps, or emails, have students print and cut and paste the material into a personal notebook. Ask them to color in the notebook or add any other content that helps them cope with negativity and anxiety. If they can't physically place it in the notebook, have them journal about the compliment.

I began doing this in my first year as an educational leader. I found the exercise uplifting and empowering. I often flipped through my positivity notebook, especially when my anxiety got the best of me. It was a way of making the negative comments weigh less and the positive ones metastasize. Using the voices of others to find your voice is an excellent exercise for students with anxiety. Like Stuart Smalley reciting his daily affirmations on *Saturday Night Live*, my positivity notebook was a way to remind my anxiety that "I'm good enough. I'm smart enough. And gosh darn it, people like me." Say it enough, and it becomes your truth.

- **Let students use manipulatives in class.** When students get anxious, they become overwhelmed with nervous energy. Without an outlet, that energy starts to work against them, and the anxiety increases. Combating anxiety is all about redirecting that energy into an effort the students can control. Manipulatives are healthy outlets for students with anxiety because they redirect nervous energy and allow for creativity, which leads to an engaged mind. When the mind is engaged, anxiety is at bay.

  When my anxiety increases, I love to play with my son. I love playing with his blocks, building with his Legos, and making city layouts with his cars and trucks. These aren't commercial manipulatives, such as Fidget Spinners, but they work just as effectively. Add blocks and other manipulatives to a creativity corner in your classroom. Giving students the ability to advocate for themselves and use the corner to curb their anxiety gives them control in an otherwise powerless environment.

MOVING FORWARD

Student voice is becoming a buzz phrase in education. We often hear it discussed when talking about relevance and student engagement in the classroom. While these are aspects of an effective learning environment, student voice is also absolutely essential. For those suffering from anxiety, student voice *is* self-advocacy.

For many students, making their voice heard comes naturally, but for those with anxiety, it does not. Educators must encourage student voice and make the classroom feel less like the teacher's and more like the students'. Charlotte and Andrew were successful in allowing student voice to drive their classroom. Students with anxiety felt comfortable and successful in their class, even though there were fifty-six students in the room.

But the situation in Charlotte and Andrew's classroom was not the average experience for students with anxiety. Too often, they don't have a voice in the classroom and can't advocate for themselves. Andrea was a student struggling with severe anxiety, but her mom, Tina, was the one communicating with her teachers. This created a situation in which Andrea was incapable of advocating for herself.

Family members of those struggling with anxiety want to help their children, but advocating for them is not helping, it's hurting. Educators need to provide students with opportunities to grow into their own advocates. Rather than focusing on reaching the end of the curriculum, focus on the students themselves. Be emotionally available for your students. Make the classroom feel smaller and promote creativity. Converse with your students, conference with them one on one to build relationships, and verbalize what the eighty-two on their assignment means. Teach students how to be mindful and use their hands to manipulate and gain control over their extra energy.

These strategies will help students like Andrea learn to understand their anxiety better and communicate their struggles and needs on their own. They will also give someone like Michael an activity to look forward to, making school a safer place.

If school is a place to provide students with the skills necessary to be successful at the next level, then we need to teach them how to read their emotions and determine what to do when they need help. Self-advocacy is an essential life skill, and it's time to promote it in our classrooms to help students with anxiety cope inside and outside of school.

THINK **ABOUT** IT

1. In what ways can you make your classroom feel smaller?

2. How can you design lessons so you are a facilitator rather than a "talking head"?

3. In what ways can you incorporate creativity, design, and building into your school or classroom?

Encourage Effort

Increase Perseverance by Removing Labels from Students with Anxiety

I am so smart. I am so smart. I am so smart. I am
so smart. S–M–R–T. I mean S–M–A–R–T.
— HOMER SIMPSON, AMERICAN TV CARTOON ICON

ANXIETY IS A diagnosis. It's a label that can make it difficult to overcome adversity, to fight back. Certain labels are unavoidable: assistant principal, mother, father, all-star, pro bowler, teacher. But many labels are given to us without formality; they're categories in which we group each other without sufficient data. You ride a bike? You're a biker. You got a 90 on your spelling test? You're smart. You make your friends laugh sometimes? You're a comedian.

The problem with labels is that even with the best intentions, they can pigeonhole us. Labels create expectations, and because they aren't self-imposed expectations, they are often impossible for us to live up to. Having anxiety is difficult enough; it's a diagnosis that takes a while to accept. But having to live up to other labels on top of that can be debilitating.

To support students with anxiety, educators need to understand why labels are harmful, what labels are being used, and how we can eliminate them from our schools and classrooms quickly and efficiently. Being a great educator and leading forward isn't about making big changes; it's about recognizing the little things and making the necessary changes to allow for the greatest possible student success.

I'm Not a Runner

I began my journey toward emotional well-being decades ago, after my initial diagnosis. I started with counseling, followed by medication. But the journey wasn't a straight, clear path to where I am today. I didn't have a trail map. There were lefts and rights, uphills and downhills. Sometimes the path was barely visible and I had to bushwhack my way through the overgrowth to find a clearing. It wasn't until I found that clearing of movement and exercise that I seemed to stay on the path more easily. Sure, there were, and still are, times when the path narrows and the vegetation tickles my ankles, but by putting one foot in front of the other, most days, the path naturally seems to widen.

This doesn't happen because I am a good hiker, or a clinical therapist. It happens because I press on and fight through the challenges. In fact, I am not much for titles like hiker, or therapist, or in the case of my exercise, runner. These labels all have a finality to them that makes me feel like I have no room left to grow. But we always have room to grow; life is never final as long as we are living.

I started running in October of 2016. I was home on maternity leave with my second child, and I was tired of merely being a mother. Please understand: I was enjoying my time with my baby girl, but I was just not interested in sitting around the house, even when I had time to myself.

As the story goes, I threw on my two-year-old pair of $40 cross trainers and set out to run a mile around my neighborhood. At the time, I knew it wasn't a small goal, but I thought it was attainable. Fourteen minutes later, I proved it was. But a fourteen-minute mile is nothing to write home about. The point was, I did it, and I had room for improvement.

> *Being a great educator and leading forward isn't about making big changes; it's about recognizing the little things and making the necessary changes to allow for the greatest possible student success.*

Since that day, I have committed to keeping up with running and working out again. I had begun working with a personal trainer in 2014, less than a year after the birth of my first child, but had stopped after learning of my second pregnancy. I suffered from severe and intense postpartum depression with my son, and discovered that exercise helped me get to a better place emotionally. It helped with my depression—and with my ongoing anxiety. Because of that, I committed to getting active again, and this time, I was going to supplement the cross-training with running.

Although I had never completed a road race, I always dreamed of running the Boston Marathon. Growing up just south of the city and watching it on television every Patriot's Day, I was inspired. I decided to run my first road race, a 5K, on April 1, 2017. I managed to finish in just over thirty minutes. Eventually, I started running a road race every month between April and November. (I may be a born New Englander, but I refuse to run outside in the cold.)

I've completed five half marathons (my best time was 2:03), ran a sub-twenty-five-minute 5K, and a sub-fifty-four-minute 10K. For all of my running accomplishments, my running partner and I still disagree on one major point: am I a runner?

Typically, I give in because she just won't accept my arguments, but I don't call myself a runner. Perhaps it seems like a semantic argument, but for me, it's not. It's an argument of identity, of effort, of heart, and anxiety.

I'm not a runner. I'm a fighter, someone with a mental illness who takes to the streets, or the treadmill, to work on fighting against the anxiety that fills my body and mind. I'm not a runner; I'm someone who happens to run. This mentality allows me to get through the challenges in every run I take. When I am on a run that isn't going well, which is often, if I called myself a runner, my mental discourse would be negative, and focused on why I was failing. The voice of my anxiety would win, reminding me that I am not a good enough runner, and never will be. My anxiety would have proof right in front of its face.

On the other hand, when I am on a run that isn't going well, and I call myself a fighter, I figure out how to get to the finish line. I cut through the pain and find the positive in the situation. I tell my anxiety that every step I take is one step closer to my goal and that I am going to win over the anxiety. If I called myself a runner, and I encountered another streak of bad runs like I did in the summer of 2019, I might never lace up my sneakers again. So no, I am not a runner, because that's what my anxiety wants. I'm a mom of two, an educator, and a driven professional with guts and a will to keep going … who happens to run a couple of times a week. (If you're a teacher who also likes to run, you'll find running and teaching insights combined in *Chasing Greatness: 26.2 Ways Teaching Is Like Running a Marathon* by Mike Roberts, also published by Times 10.)

LEAD **FORWARD** STRATEGY
Celebrate Effort, Not Smarts

When we label students, we run the risk of destroying their sense of self and eliminating any intrinsic motivation or perseverance they may have. Students may not balk at a label in the beginning, but at some point, they may come to feel like they can't live up to the title anymore. For students with anxiety, this is inevitable; their anxiety convinces them they aren't what people think they are and they give up. If I were a runner, my times wouldn't consistently be getting worse from one race to the other. If I were smart, long division wouldn't be so difficult.

Celebrating smarts is likely to increase anxiety, rather than reduce it. It's essentially teaching students to have a fixed mindset, and that's the last type of mindset a student with anxiety needs. Carol Dweck, a psychology professor at Stanford University, studies human motivation and teaches that a fixed mindset is believing that your intelligence, personality, and moral character are predetermined and thus unchangeable. This means that students with anxiety will spend their time trying to prove how smart they are—that they have those predetermined smarts—rather than learning from their mistakes. When trying to prove yourself, missteps along the way look like failure. Students with anxiety already deal with the fear of failure often enough. We have to find a way to cut at least one possibility from that list.

Encouraging effort and helping students learn from their mistakes, Dweck explains, teaches and supports a growth mindset rather than a fixed, labeled mindset. "The growth mindset," she says, "is based on the belief that your basic qualities are things you can cultivate through your efforts." So how can we support students with anxiety without giving them labels?

- **Encourage them.** Encouragement can go a long way—
  even further than you expect. If encouragement was an
  investment, it would have the biggest return. The effort
  it takes to encourage a student with anxiety is minimal
  compared to the positive impact it has on the student's
  emotions. When we encourage students, even during
  small tasks, it helps them manage their anxieties. An
  accomplishment might seem inconsequential to us, but
  to the person who accomplished it, it could be a big
  deal. Maybe the teacher didn't notice that Johnny col-
  laborated with Shane on his six fraction problems and
  even asked Shane a couple of questions. But to Johnny,
  being able to ask a classmate a question was an accomplishment. Typically, his anxiety is so intense that he
  can't ask his peers questions because he's afraid they'll
  think he's not smart.

  If that is the case, imagine how empowering it would
  be for him to hear his teacher say, "Great job collaborating
  with Shane on this. Keep using the resources around you
  that you're comfortable with. Awesome job." It confirms
  that he did great by stepping out of his comfort level, and
  confirms that he can and should do it again.

  Encouraging students doubles the score instanta-
  neously: Johnny, 2. Johnny's anxiety, 0. And it works
  to get rid of any label they might have thought they
  were wearing. Kids who had been labeled incapable of
  working with others suddenly feel that they can step
  outside of that box. After every one-on-one interaction with your students, leave them with a positive
  encouragement. No matter why the check-in happened, whether to correct a concerning behavior or an

academic mistake, always end the conversation by high-lighting what they're doing well.

- **Replace "You're so smart" with "You're working so hard."** At my house, we constantly say, "You're working so hard." No matter what my six- or three-year-olds are eager to show me: a score of 100 on a paper at school, a backhanded shot while playing hockey in the garage, or cleaning up after dinner by putting their plate in the sink without help, I always praise my kids with, "Wow, you are working so hard. Keep it up!" I never say, "Wow, you're so smart," or "Wow, you're such a good hockey player," or even, "Wow, you're so strong." I want to encourage effort and hard work, not smarts, skills, or strength. All of those are too absolute, with no room for improvement. What happens the next time my son struggles at school or on the ice? Is he going to give up because he thinks there's no room for improvement, and that the struggle proves that he's not enough? Or is he going to persevere because he "works so hard," and he knows Mommy is going to acknowledge that?

   Teaching is no different. The more educators recognize and praise the hard work and efforts of their students, the more likely the students will be to continue fighting their anxiety when they're faced with challenges. Every accomplishment is more than an accomplishment in mathematics, or sports, or everyday chores; it's an accomplishment in fighting anxiety—that inner voice constantly doubting their ability, their smarts, their skills, and their strength.

- **Be proud of their commitment.** Most students will tell you that the worst feeling in the world isn't when their parents are mad at them, but when their parents are disappointed in them. The same is true when you talk to a student about their teachers and coaches. But if students will tell you that knowing the adults in their lives are disappointed with them is the worst feeling in the world, they will also tell you that it's the best feeling in the world when those same adults are proud of them.

For students with anxiety, it's crushing when someone is disappointed in them; it's almost incapacitating. They, more than others, need to know the adults in their lives are proud of them; it tells them that they haven't done anything wrong.

Be proud of the commitment all your students make to their academics, extracurriculars, and themselves, regardless of outcomes, but be especially proud of those with anxiety. Telling a student you are proud of them is the best encouragement you can give. If we are going to prioritize small, attainable goals, we must communicate the pride we feel for students with anxiety when they accomplish them. Use some of the following statements regularly in your classroom: "I'm proud of how hard you worked on this assignment." "I'm proud of you for working through the material without giving up." "I'm proud of you for collaborating with your classmate on this." "I'm proud of you for asking for help."

Every time you let your students with anxiety know you are proud of them, you energize them to continue to fight through their illness.

Numerical Labels

In the middle of my twelfth year in the classroom, I decided to make a drastic change to how I graded my students on assessments. I had been teaching AP biology for nearly ten years and I wasn't making any gains in effectively using assessments to prepare students for the AP exam in May. In addition, the negative impact assessments had on my students with anxiety was doing more harm than good. All of my students were hard workers, so it wasn't that they were failing to prepare. I tried it all—shortening the duration of a testing session and adjusting the types of questions I asked—but my students with anxiety still struggled. Their comments about testing in my classroom sounded like this:

"Oh, great, another test. I'm gonna fail again."

"I used to be an A student, and then I took these tests, and now I'm a D student."

"I don't even study anymore. I fail all the time."

"According to this class, I'm a bad student, but I study all the time."

After years of hearing student comments like these, I came to a deep realization: tests were labeling my students. For students with anxiety, all my assessments did was give them a numerical label they could never overcome.

54: "You're a failure."

66: "Bad at biology."

72: "You're just like everyone else: average."

I had to eliminate those labels for my students with anxiety, and I was determined to do so. My thinking was as follows: learning to ride a bike is a common experience in childhood. The traditional path to success begins with a tricycle or big wheel, then you ride a bike with training wheels, and finally, one day, those training wheels come off and you ... fall over as soon as you try to ride. Does that mean you're a bad bike rider?

Depending on the individual, it can take a couple tries to ride without training wheels: a day, a couple of days, or even longer. But what is the end goal? The idea is that we learn to ride a bike, correct? When we reminisce about learning to ride a bike, we rarely talk about how long it took us to learn or how old we were. We simply talk about whether or not we can ride. No one labels us based on our first attempt, because the expectation is that we aren't going to be successful the first time. We work our way through the difficulties, find out how to adjust when our balance is off, and eventually learn how to ride a bike.

I decided to make a drastic change and remove the numerical labels that tests were putting on my students with anxiety.

"Alright everyone, I'm going to pass back your evolution tests now," I announced.

An audible grumble in unison filled the room as if it were a choir rehearsal.

"I failed," Megan announced with laughter.

"I'm so bad at biology," giggled John.

"Everyone stop," I demanded. "What you see for a grade on the test right now will no longer be your grade on the assessment." Instantly I had the attention of the whole class. It was as if I sent a "We need to talk" text; it instantly made their collective hearts sink.

"What do you mean?" asked Megan.

"I'll explain. You're going to take your tests home and be able to rework them on your own. I will schedule three days after school for you and a classmate to make an appointment with me. You will come after school and talk me through every question you got wrong, what the correct answer is, and why it is the correct answer. You will then earn your points back on the exam."

"So we don't have to write anything down?" Megan asked.

"You can bring all the notes you want with you, though I'm not going to collect them. If it were me, I would go through the test, rework the questions, make a note of the correct answers, and then figure out how to explain the question or problem verbally. If you want to make notes on how to explain it and bring them with you, that's great."

"So wait, we have to meet one on one with you and talk to you about the test? What happens if we are wrong?"

"Then we talk through it. Look, the point is that you need to learn the material. Learning from your mistakes is just as valuable, if not more so, than getting it right the first time. I am tired of hearing you all talk so negatively about yourselves over these exams. Plus, you're not learning from them. Sometimes I repeat questions on the tests and you get them wrong a second and third time. If you were learning the material, you wouldn't be getting the questions wrong again, right?"

The class's lack of a response was the only confirmation I needed.

"So here is the sign-up sheet. Figure out who you are going to work with and put your names on the paper. You have three dates with five time slots as your options. Pick one."

The class immediately started talking to each other, and one at a time, the time slots filled up. I was all in, and so were they.

I delivered my new approach to testing with the utmost confidence, but on the inside, I could only dream of its success. I had no idea whether the change was going to improve test scores, reduce anxiety, or prepare students more effectively for the AP exam. What it ended up doing was not only accomplishing all three, but also changing the climate and culture of my classroom. Students were not only talking to me about the content, they were collaborating with each other. They would gather outside my office just before an appointment and talk to each other about questions, explaining to one another why the answers were correct. Students were engaged and collaborating. They didn't want to disappoint me by not being prepared.

As for any potential anxiety surrounding having to meet and talk to the teacher, the students quickly rose above it. The meetings became conversations pertaining to far more than just the AP biology curriculum. It was a bonding time, and we conversed in an authentic way. We laughed, we joked, we even cried. The time we spent working on "test corrections" helped us form positive personal relationships. Tests went from being labeled by my students with anxiety as something they couldn't fight (a failure, bad at biology, not a hard worker), to a time in which real, authentic teaching and learning occurred. The grade was a checkpoint, an indication of how much they knew as of that date. It allowed them to see what they needed to focus on. I removed the finality of the assessment and instead made hard work and effort the focal point—two qualities that we should celebrate, not stifle, for our students with anxiety.

LEAD **FORWARD** STRATEGY
Rethink Grading

Grading practices are a hot-button topic in education. Conversations about them can lead to passionate disagreement and dissent. I am not here to tell educators how to grade, or even what best grading practices are; however, I am here to say that for many students, grades exacerbate anxiety by labeling our students.

Grades create a fear of failure in students, not because of the number that appears at the top of the paper, but because of the finality of the grade and the label it gives the student. The number says, "You're not smart enough," or "You didn't try hard enough." It doesn't say, "Good job, you already know 63 percent of the material, keep working hard." I failed the first time I tried to ride my bike. My grade would have been a zero because I fell almost instantly, or a five because I stayed up for five seconds before falling. Do these grades mean I wouldn't get another chance?

We have to rethink grading to reflect growth and develop confidence, rather than allowing them to create anxiety in our students. Try these strategies for eliminating the numerical labels that grades place on students.

- **Allow corrections.** Is the goal for the student to learn the content by a certain date, or is the goal for the student to learn the content, period? My most valuable learning has come from the errors I made, not from figuring out what the "formula" for success was and implementing it from the get-go. In an exercise I participated in years ago, I was asked to select a grading philosophy from a list of six of the most common ones. From that list, the majority of educators at the table selected the philosophy that defined grading as a way to assess how much of a concept a student knew. It was not a mechanism by which to punish students for not learning material by a certain point or in a certain way, but that's what it becomes. That's the way students with anxiety see it.

  Academia is a place to teach students, not punish them. Allowing students to learn at a pace that is comfortable for them communicates the idea that they aren't failing, but rather just not there *yet*. The makers of *Sesame Street* were so impressed with the *Power of Yet* that they made a song about it. That song has over 116 million views on YouTube. Think of it this way: if you were going to start running, I wouldn't give you a week and then ask you to run a 5K, only to comment that you didn't work hard enough because you couldn't break the thirty-minute mark. You may not be able to reach the goal yet, but you will if you keep working hard.

Assignment corrections are essential for students, especially those with anxiety. It tells the students that they didn't fail, but that they're not there *yet*. It allows them to work and celebrate their efforts, as opposed to their smarts. I didn't care if two students got the same grade and one earned it the first time through, and the other earned it after making corrections. Every time I fell off my bike, I made a correction and tried again, and school should be no different.

Start by coming up with a method for assignment corrections. I found that corrections that excluded student/teacher discourse didn't work. Students just wanted to finish them to get a better grade. They just wanted to change the label. But remember, we are trying to get the students to *learn*. Once you establish a protocol for corrections, implement it. You will see more academic success—and less anxiety—from your students.

- **Get rid of red.** Red communicates intense feelings: power, anger, passion, or danger. Yet red is the color in which many teachers provide feedback and grades. As a student, I remember feeling powerless when I got an assignment or test back from a teacher and it had red all over it. Each mark and comment felt like it was going to follow me forever, like there was nothing I could possibly do to change it. The red didn't feel like a conversation or feedback; it felt like a conclusion.

  That powerlessness increases anxiety and feelings of inadequacy. It doesn't open the door to self-advocacy. Students are likely to see the grade, swallow the inadvertent message it sends, and physically move on to the next assignment. The simplicity of choosing to grade student work and providing feedback in a color other than red can change all that. It subconsciously communicates to students that you're eliminating that label—and that will likely increase their effort. It says to a student with anxiety that you are there to work with them, not judge them on their abilities.

- **Make a note of the points earned, not lost.** If the philosophy of grading is to indicate where students are relative to a standard, why do we focus on what they weren't able to accomplish? How does pointing out where they went wrong give them an incentive to improve? When I stopped using red, I also changed how I graded exams. Rather than scoring students by indicating the points lost on a question, I noted the points gained. Questions from students went from, "Why is this wrong?" to "What am I missing here?" The former felt confrontational, the latter, inquisitive.

  Open up the lines of communication with your students with anxiety. Do whatever you can to help promote rather than discourage. Seeing +2 on a paper feels so much better than seeing -1. Change your perspective and focus on the positive, and you'll send a message to students with anxiety that they're not going to be perfect all the time, but there are always positive accomplishments that deserve their attention. Stop scoring assessments based on points lost. Start scoring by showing students all the points they *earned*.

MOVING FORWARD

Life is full of challenges, both physical and mental. For students with anxiety, even the simplest tasks can be challenges, thanks to the constant feelings of inadequacy, fear, and lack of control. Every day is a struggle and a fight. Students with anxiety need teachers who are going to celebrate accomplishments and effort, rather than label them and potentially pass judgment. Celebrating effort means encouraging students, telling them when they are working hard, and communicating how proud you are of their efforts. It does not mean using statements like "You're so smart," or "You're great at math." These statements might be made with the best of intentions as a way to encourage the students to feel good about themselves. But instead, they are keeping students with anxiety from being able to persevere when they start to struggle.

We also need to consider the labels that grades put on our students with anxiety. Educators can rethink grades and provide additional opportunities for students to show they've met learning outcomes. Letting students with anxiety know what points they've earned rather than lost, and getting rid of the red pen when grading, are other strategies that will make students with anxiety feel less like failures and more capable of fighting through difficult material and situations.

Small changes like these might seem inconsequential, but the subtle messages they communicate can make all the difference in the world. The first time a student with anxiety tries to ride a bike and falls, they are already thinking, "I'm the world's worst bike rider. I suck at this. I am never going to learn how to do it." Giving them a note in red that says "5 percent" at the top and immediately moving onto skateboarding isn't going to change that internal dialogue. It confirms it. The only way I have been able to accomplish the task of authoring this book—which has brought me high anxiety—is to call myself a hard worker, not an author.

For more details about how to remove the labels and empower students with open dialogue, reflection, and self-evaluation, see the book *Hacking Assessment: 10 Ways to Go Gradeless in a Traditional Grades School*, by Starr Sackstein.

Eliminate titles and labels from our students with anxiety, and you will empower them to keep fighting.

THINK **ABOUT** IT

1. How can you remove labels and encourage effort in your classroom or school?

2. What is your philosophy on grading, and do your grading practices reflect your philosophy?

3. What changes can you make in your grading policies/practices tomorrow that will curb student anxieties related to grades and better reflect your philosophies?

CHAPTER 9

Maintain Routines

Establish Clear and Consistent Routines in the Classroom for Your Anxious Students' Bodies and Minds

Depending on what they are, our habits will either make us or break us. We become what we repeatedly do.
— SEAN COVEY, AMERICAN BUSINESS EXECUTIVE

ONE OF THE most effective strategies for managing my anxiety through the years has been to create routines for myself and stick to them. My routines are intense, from the time I wake up, to the foods I eat, and when. To some, my processes might be too rigid, but they are effective and necessary for controlling my anxiety.

Anxiety feeds off of dead air and unpredictable situations. When students with anxiety have too much unscheduled time on their hands, their minds make up for it and work overtime, increasing their anxiety and self-doubt with every passing minute. When these students become dependent on routines and a variable threatens to throw them off, their anxiety flourishes. Instead, we must create as many predictable routines as possible. Support students with anxiety by creating routines in the classroom, prioritizing the routines of their bodies/physiology, and helping them re-establish routines slowly when they are thrown off.

You'll see an immediate reduction in their anxiety and panic attacks.

Living Up to the Expectations of a Legend

Mr. Goodwin was an award-winning educator. He was a math teacher at the local public high school, and an icon in town. He was named National Teacher of the Year twice and coached the high school math team to multiple national championships.

His teaching strategies were different, and at a time when there was no technology in the classroom, he was advanced. He didn't use a textbook, and his students were never given published worksheets. Rather, Mr. Goodwin wrote every problem on his own that his students ever did—including exams—in the context of what he'd gone over with the students in a given "unit." There were no multiple-choice questions in his classes. His tests were organic and unannounced.

The material Mr. Goodwin taught was not organized into traditional unit plans. Students would go over problems, work with classmates, and then one day, unbeknownst to them, walk into class to see blank white paper already placed on each desk. Those days were test days.

Not announcing exams was a unique approach. Sure, students took pop quizzes in other classes, but pop unit tests? Mr. Goodwin explained that his rationale for not telling students when they were going to have a test was that he believed you should always be prepared. It was the same reason why he never checked homework. It was assigned, students did it, and hopefully did well on tests as a result. If students chose not to do their homework, well, then they'd look foolish when Mr. Goodwin called on them in class. They also wouldn't do well on the exams.

Mr. Goodwin taught advanced math courses. Students placed in his freshman class continued on a track that saw them placed into his subsequent classes for their remaining three years. His teaching philosophy was a hardline approach that saw his freshman classes of twenty-five-plus whittled down to fewer than fifteen by senior year. To be a senior in Mr. Goodwin's class was an accomplishment in and of itself. The lessons he taught went far beyond mathematics; he taught students about strength, perseverance, and determination, but at what cost?

Students had Mr. Goodwin on their radar as early as sixth grade, and it was no different for Brian. He was the third of three boys, and his two older brothers were both products of Mr. Goodwin's math classes. Each saw great success both in his classes and as members of the math team. As a freshman, Brian was placed into Mr. Goodwin's advanced math class, along with twenty-five other students. Academically, he had the same potential as his brothers, but emotionally, he struggled with anxiety that up to that point he'd been managing.

Brian felt as prepared as possible heading into the first day of school. He knew, by way of his brothers, that for the first day of school, he needed to memorize the squares from one through thirty and the square roots from one through nine hundred, because Mr. Goodwin was going to verbally quiz the class about them. It was essential to make a good first impression and curb his anxiety as much as possible.

Brian studied and memorized his numbers all summer. On the first day, he sat in the last row, as far from Mr. Goodwin as physically possible, and thought it unlikely he'd be put on the spot. Regardless, he was prepared, or so he thought. Brian knew what to expect: no textbook, no excuses, no fear. But once he was sitting in front of Mr. Goodwin, all bets were off. His presence was more intimidating than Brian had expected. Sure, Mr. Goodwin was in his seventies and no taller than five-foot-six, but he was the biggest man in town, never mind the classroom.

"What's the square root of 256? Brian?"

"Me?"

"No, the other Brian in here. Yes, you, Mr. Williamson."

Brian started to panic; his palms became sweaty. "Umm, fifteen?"

"Is that a question or an answer, Mr. Williamson?"

"An answer?" His mind was racing. Was the answer not fifteen? No, it was fifteen. He knew that.

"Were you daydreaming, Mr. Williamson?"

"No."

Mr. Goodwin turned his back to the class. "Okay, then what color is my tie?"

Brian was silent for a moment, now visibly sweating.

"Mr. Williamson, are you still with me?"

"Yes."

"The color of my tie, Mr. Williamson?"

"Ummm, blue?"

"Question or an answer, Mr. Williamson?"

"Answer."

Mr. Goodwin turned around. "It's red, Mr. Williamson. You've been watching me for what, thirty minutes so far, and you weren't paying close enough attention to know the color of my tie?"

"Sorry." Brian couldn't think straight. His heart was pounding and his mind was racing.

"No sorry, Mr. Williamson. The square root of 256, Mr. Williamson?"

"Fifteen."

"Answer?"

"Yes, an answer."

"You need to learn your square roots, Mr. Williamson. I will ask you again tomorrow. David?"

"Sixteen."

"Correct."

Mr. Goodwin immediately turned and continued teaching at the board.

Brian didn't know what hit him. He'd known the answer was sixteen, so why did he say fifteen? He was so overwhelmed; his anxiety was taking over his whole body. He had to do more to prepare. If he couldn't perform such a simple task, how was he ever going to overcome the larger obstacles that lay ahead?

Brian's experience on the first day in Mr. Goodwin's class, unfortunately, didn't change much through the first month. Daily at lunch, just before class, he would get himself so worked up over whether or not he'd be walking into a test that he couldn't calm himself down enough in class to fully focus and comprehend the math. He was spending so much energy fighting the anxiety over what he was going to walk into that he wasn't able to perform. He fought his emotions as much as possible, but when he finally did walk into his first test, he was so overcome with anxiety that the material on the exam looked foreign. He didn't feel good about his performance, and the anxiety didn't stop there. Now he was thinking about what would happen the day he got his test back.

Mr. Goodwin didn't grade in a traditional manner, either. Rather than giving a test back with a percentage at the top, he simply put a circled number at the top of the front page. The number indicated the number of points lost on the test. The class would then have to sit and wait for him to put the scoring scale on the board to determine their grade, and, not surprisingly, it was never the same. Sometimes 0–5 was an A, sometimes 0–13 was an A. Brian was reeling; he never knew when there was a test, and he never knew how he did when he got his test back. Mr. Goodwin was in control of it all, and Brian was in control of nothing, not even his anxiety.

After fighting intense anxiety for the first month in Mr. Goodwin's class, Brian knew he wasn't going to be able to keep it up for four years. Considering this, along with finding out he failed the first exam, led him to an important decision. He became the first of eleven students to drop out of Mr. Goodwin's class before reaching sophomore year. The constant wondering when he'd be called on in class, when there would be a test, and what the number at the top of the paper meant when he got a test back was more than he could handle. The lack of routine exacerbated his anxiety.

Educators need to establish classroom routines that help students understand expectations. When students with anxiety know what is expected of them, they can make adjustments to manage their anxiety and try to work through their difficulties. When a teacher provides stability to students with anxiety, the students feel like they are winning even more control. When it comes to anxious students, we need to be explicit about our classroom routines—and we need to maintain that consistency.

LEAD **FORWARD** STRATEGY
Implement Routines

Mr. Goodwin was a legend, an anomaly. He taught in a way that in my thirty-three years in education (seventeen as a student and sixteen as a professional), I have never seen again. He was an award-winning teacher, so his approach worked, but he also taught at a time when you either conformed and suffered in silence, or dropped the class, much like Brian.

For four years, I somehow found a way to conform to Mr.

Goodwin's approach and suffer in silence. However, this neither means that I was managing my anxiety well, nor that a teaching approach like Mr. Goodwin's would be successful today. With the knowledge we now have about anxiety in schools, Mr. Goodwin's class would be even more exclusive than it was over twenty years ago. The lack of consistency and routine in his class, regardless of how iconic a teacher he was, would not work for most anxious students, not with all of the other pressures students in the twenty-first century experience.

Provide consistent structure, even in the form of unit layouts, and you can reduce the number of anxiety triggers. You can help to eliminate anxiety's hold on students' lives.

Mr. Goodwin made me fight my anxiety every single day. His class was always unknown and unpredictable. I constantly doubted myself and compared myself to the perceived preparedness of my classmates. Every day, I had lunch just before Mr. Goodwin's class, and my classmates and I spent twenty-five minutes surveying each other as to the likelihood that we'd walk into a test. I couldn't even take twenty-five minutes to enjoy lunch. Students with anxiety need routine. They need consistency and structure if they are going to focus academically and find success in the classroom.

- **Develop unit structure.** No matter your teaching style, students with anxiety benefit from consistency. What used to look like teacher-directed instruction for days followed by a traditional assessment has changed dramatically. That said, teachers can still set up their curriculum so that students know what to expect for every unit. For example, in my AP classes, each unit of study, regardless of content, was two to three weeks in length. They began with self-directed research, followed by class discussions and learning activities, and all of it culminated in at least three days of inquiry-based lab work. Students knew what the unit assessments were before we began: a group lab presentation and a unit test. The material changed—i.e., questions and activity specifics—but the structure did not.

Students with anxiety have only their anxiety on which to rely; it becomes a love/hate relationship. Provide consistent structure, even in the form of unit layouts, and you can reduce the number of anxiety triggers. You can help to eliminate anxiety's hold on students' lives.

Start by working backward and coming up with a skeleton of what you'd like units to look like. What are the major activities or tasks you want students to engage in during each unit? Once you've established these major activities/tasks, decide how much time you want to dedicate to each. This will give you a sense of the average total length of a unit. From here, commit to what you've established. Of course, you'll find situations where you have to change, but a day or two here or there isn't a big deal. I experienced times when a lab inquiry only took two days as opposed to three, or when I thought my students needed additional instruction to support a lesson. You can manipulate the timing as long as you maintain the overall unit structure expectations.

- **Provide a weekly agenda.** Daily agendas not only create well-structured lessons, but also communicate expectations. Whenever I walk into a classroom to observe, I look for an agenda that students can see for the duration of the lesson. But why stop at a daily agenda? Unless you are a first-year teacher, or someone who is teaching a course for the first time, you're probably planning in advance. Sure, you might not know the intricacies of each day's lesson, but you probably have an idea of the majority of the week, or even the unit.

Why not share this plan with students?

Weekly agendas allow students to plan ahead and manage their time. Include assignment due dates, lab activities, and daily lesson objectives, if and when appropriate. Present the weekly agenda each Monday. Every day thereafter, start each class by drawing students' attention to the weekly agenda. Review it, reinforce assignment dates, and make any necessary adjustments.

Although one might argue that seeing a week's worth of work in advance might be anxiety-inducing for students, it prevents surprises and allows students to implement many of the other strategies discussed thus far: setting small, attainable goals; prioritizing self-advocacy; and implementing the fifteen-minute rule, just to name a few.

AP Biology
Mon 09-18 to Friday 09-22
(This example shows three days from a weekly agenda.)

Wed 09-20: Students will be able to present experiments designed and conducted to test the effects of environmental conditions on reaction rate of an enzyme & be able to analyze a set of data.

- Finish Lab Presentations
- Essays: 2013, 7 & 2016, 8 (15 minutes total)
- Score Classmate's Essays with Rubric

Homework:

1. Macromolecules Chart due FRIDAY 09/22
2. TEST Unit 1: *Chemistry of Life* FRIDAY 09/22 – MONDAY 09/25
3. Unit 2: Cells Study Guide NOTES due TUESDAY 9/26 → QUIZ

Thurs 09-21: Students will be able to show understanding of enzymes by scoring at least a 5/10 on two FRQ in the time given and peer edit responses according to the AP scoring rubric.

- Essays: 2013, 7 & 2016, 8 (15 minutes total)
- Score Classmate's Essays with Rubric
- Macromolecules Chart

Homework:

1. Macromolecules Chart due TOMORROW
2. TEST Unit 1: *Chemistry of Life* MONDAY 09/25
3. Unit 2: Cells Study Guide NOTES due TUESDAY 09/26 → QUIZ

Fri 09-22: Students will be able to score at least a 75 on a test about the Chemistry of Life.

- Collect Macromolecules Chart
- TEST Unit 1: *Chemistry of Life* GRID IN & ESSAY

Homework:

1. TEST Unit 1: *Chemistry of Life* MONDAY 09-25
2. Unit 2: Cells Study Guide NOTES due TUESDAY 09/26 → QUIZ

Image 9.1: An effective weekly agenda like this one can make all the difference for kids with anxiety because it eliminates surprises and incorporates attainable goals along the way.

- **Design well-structured lessons.** Routine needs to exist, not just within a unit, or a week, but in every class day. Students should know what to expect each time they walk into the classroom. This begins with an agenda, whether written on the board daily, or reviewed weekly. Begin class this way, and you will set the stage for the duration of your time together. Additionally, give each lesson an objective: what is it that you want students to accomplish as a result of what you will be doing together? This objective tells students with anxiety the end goal and the why—and both can help to reduce anxiety and maintain focus on the learning process. Once you've established the agenda and objectives, keep the remainder of the lesson flowing and building up to the end goal. Students with anxiety want to be in control; that is never going to change. If you can show them exactly what they'll be doing in any given unit, they'll be able to give up that control without causing themselves additional anxiety. Give them a well-structured lesson, and they'll believe that you have a plan. From there, they will be able to let *you* have control.

That Gut Feeling

It was another Sunday night, and I was in the midst of yet another grueling stomachache. I'd felt fine all day, but within a half-hour of eating dinner, I was doubled over with intense cramping. It always seemed to happen at the most inconvenient times. It was after 7 p.m. and I had to start preparing for the week. I never stayed up past 10 p.m. and I still had homework and studying to complete. I didn't have time to tend to a vicious stomachache.

But this had become a pattern for me. After spending two days on my own schedule, completing work at my own pace and without the potential for judgment, I couldn't easily wrap my mind around returning to the structure and pace of a school week. Sunday nights had become brutal. But my mother and I started looking at my diet to find a cause. Was it a particular meal or food that was upsetting my stomach? There seemed to be a connection between the upset and milk and cheese, so we figured I was lactose intolerant. I stayed away from ice cream, and my mother began purchasing over-the-counter medication to take before eating dairy, all to fend off any potential stomach upset.

The plan seemed to work for a while, but the pills' effectiveness was inconsistent at best. I convinced myself that it was all in the timing: taking the medication ten minutes before a meal, or thirty seconds before, could mean the difference between pain so intense I'd be in tears, or cramping that I could fight through. I knew I was feeling overwhelmed about the change in schedules from the weekend to the school week, but had no idea that the overwhelm could be the root of the problem.

As time went on, my mother and I worked harder to troubleshoot my ailment, although it got worse. I started having intense cramping in the mornings before school. The more I suffered, the larger the list of "can't haves" got. But the longer the list became, the more inconsistent my symptoms were. The cramping would subside and then I would go for days, sometimes a week or more, without being able to go to the bathroom. I would have trouble sleeping because, as I described to my mother, it felt like there was a brick in my stomach. Some days I was so sick that my mother would keep me home from school and pump me with laxatives to restart my system. It would work for a day, but then the cycle would start again: days of inconsistent cramping followed by days or weeks of constipation.

After months of unsuccessful treatments at home—laxatives,

warm liquids, changes to my diet, whatever my mother could think of—she decided to take me to the doctor. I sat sobbing in the examination room as I admitted to my physician the embarrassment of first having stomach cramping so bad I couldn't leave the house, to then being so constipated it hurt.

The doctor sent me for an X-ray. The technician was sweet and spoke in a soft voice as she gave me instructions about how to position myself for the images. I remember it being difficult to remain still for the required amount of time to take the pictures because my body was still shaking from crying.

"Okay, last one, hun," the tech said as she left the room to take the picture from behind the safety of the enclosed room.

It was a few minutes before she came back into the room to take the lead pad off of me and hand me the film.

"Having trouble going to the bathroom?" she asked.

I couldn't look at her, so I just nodded my head.

"You'll be okay, sweetie. The doctor is going to take care of you."

"Thanks."

"Good luck."

I walked back to my physician's office and handed the X-rays to the receptionist. She told me to take a seat and that the doctor would call me in momentarily. I sat next to my mom and waited. We didn't speak. She knew how difficult the last few months had been for me, and I was ashamed about how bad this had gotten. No words of encouragement were going to help me feel any better.

When the doctor called us in, she had the X-ray film in hand. "So, you are definitely constipated. It's so severe we can see it with a regular X-ray. Look."

The doctor slid the film into the light box on the wall and flipped the switch.

"Okay, so usually X-rays will not show soft tissue because it's not dense enough. That's why we typically only see bone. However, if you look at your X-ray, you can clearly see all of your intestines."

The doctor pointed to the X-ray, and sure enough, you could see the contours of my intestinal tract as clear as in a textbook.

"So the reason you can see everything is because you are filled with stool. This gives the intestines enough density for the X-ray to pick them up."

I started to cry again. I was disgusted, mortified. It was as bad as I thought.

"Does she need to see a specialist?" my mother asked, concerned.

"As bad as this looks, I don't believe it is going to require a solution other than over-the-counter medications. She is going to need to go on laxatives for multiple days, and then we need a plan to prevent this from happening again."

I was sobbing, almost to the point of being inconsolable.

"Hun, why are you so upset?" the doctor asked.

"I can't believe it's gotten this bad. It's embarrassing," I mustered through sobs.

"Look, I want you to know that I see this way more often than you probably think."

I lifted my head. "Really?"

"Yes. It's common in teenage girls."

For the first time, I felt ... normal.

"I have many patients who come here with the same problem. We need to clean you out and get you on a routine, and I'm here to help you do that."

I spent two weeks working to normalize my system. I had to wake up every morning at the same time, eat breakfast, and have a warm drink. Then I was expected to move, even if it was just going for a walk around the block. I had to eat a high fiber diet, so the doctor provided me with a list of foods. I was expected to return in two weeks for a checkup to see if the new routine was working.

At the follow-up appointment, the doctor listened to my stomach and asked how I was doing. She confirmed that I was improving and she was happy to hear the plan was working, but she wanted to know how I was doing emotionally. I told her I was happy to be feeling better, but I was still struggling with occasional cramping, especially on Sunday nights and before school.

"Keep to the diet and routine I gave you. When you get stressed out, it's going to go to your stomach. Watching what you eat and getting regular exercise will help keep you regular, even amidst the stress."

My stomach ailments plagued me through the rest of high school, college, and even the first five years of my educational career. I worked hard to maintain my routine, but at times it wasn't possible, or I got lazy and my routine changed. When my stomach started to cycle between upset and constipation, I would jump back into the routine my doctor put me on in high school, and my system would regulate. During my most heightened bouts of anxiety, my stomach suffered the most. The worst times were Sunday nights, the mornings after late nights in the lab or at work when I wouldn't be able to get a proper dinner, and nights before exams.

Uncertainty and change can take a physical toll on our students with anxiety. The mind and body are connected, and we need to understand the impact of emotions on our physical well-being. Changes, whether expected or unexpected, have a negative impact on how anxious students feel physically. We need to prioritize the physical needs of our anxious students. When we do, we help them regulate their systems and, in turn, support their emotional needs.

LEAD **FORWARD** STRATEGY
Prioritize the Physical Needs of Your Students

The human body is an impressive machine full of conscious thought, innate processes, and feats of great physical accomplishment. We are driven by our minds—by the ideas, hopes, dreams, and fears that consume our daily lives. But none of these must occur to sustain life. We are oblivious to digestion or absorption, dehydration synthesis or hydrolysis, the sodium-potassium pump, or gas exchange. Yet, all of these processes still take place, separate from the thoughts and interactions we have with ourselves, each other, and our environments.

The truth is, though, that the mind deeply impacts the homeostatic conditions of the body. As explained earlier, constant fear and stress bathe the body in cortisol, making it more susceptible to disease and infection as the immune system becomes drastically compromised. The body is fueled by routine and consistency. When we lack them, our bodies grow overworked, and we increase the danger of falling sick. The routine that my doctor established helped reset my body's expectations and stopped the negative impact of stress on my physiology.

Those stresses and changes had been affecting not only my mind, but also my body. I'd become so focused on my anxieties and my mind that I failed to see their impact on my body. Every Sunday night, as the pressures of the week ahead weighed heavier on my mind, my stomach suffered. Anxiety might be an illness of the mind, but it impacts the body. Educators need to remember this and implement strategies in the classroom that prioritize the health and necessary routines for the body.

- **Allow movement breaks.** This strategy is easier at the elementary level, with recess already being a part of the school day. Recess is not just crucial for student play, socialization, and physical well-being, but also for mental health. The body was meant to move. The endorphins released when the body moves increase the levels of dopamine in the brain, and cause feelings of happiness. Scheduled recess becomes routine for the body, and in turn, routine for neurotransmitters in the brain.

Older students don't have recess as part of their daily schedules. They take physical education classes to satisfy graduation requirements, but those are for curriculum requirements, not the free play students experience at recess. Furthermore, physical education is not offered every day for all students. Typically, classes are only a quarter or semester long, not a full year.

We must prioritize movement breaks within our classrooms. Add them as a consistent piece of the daily, or if more feasible, weekly agenda. Let students get up and have a class leader run a mini stretching or yoga session. Play a quick game of Simon Says. Allow students the opportunity to "play" again. Regardless of what you choose to do, prioritize a routine for the body and you will benefit the minds of your students.

- **Offer snack time.** In my transition from teacher to administrator, a big challenge was the impact the new role had on my schedule. I went from a regimented day, eating lunch at 10:30, to having no scheduled lunch and with everyone else owning my calendar. Some days, I don't even have time to eat. For individuals who suffer from anxiety, hunger exacerbates symptoms. Because the body is already fighting a battle with the mind, and therefore compromised, any other variables intensify it.

  I knew low blood sugar impacted me, but during a

session with my psychiatrist when she asked me if I was eating regularly, I realized that hunger could be triggering the problem. Students need the opportunity to access food when they need it. Sure, they all have lunch during the day, but sometimes that lunch block comes too late. Providing food in the classroom is no longer as simple as it was in the past. With the onset of life-threatening allergies, we must be vigilant about the health of the students, not only in classrooms but also in schools. However, we also must make food and water available to students who need it. The hungrier an anxious student gets, the more likely they are to have increased anxiety and panic attacks.

Work with your administration to find a way to make snacks available to your students. Start with bottles of water, and progress to safe snacks that are allowed by the school and district administration and health coordinators. Having food available to students with anxiety when they need it will reduce symptoms in the classroom.

- **Make rest an option for choice work.** During the conversation with my psychiatrist, when I learned that hunger exacerbates my anxiety, I also learned that a lack of sleep does too. Many students are entering our classrooms with too little rest. So many of them are over-scheduled, and their basic needs are not being prioritized. Our youngest students get an opportunity to nap during the school day, but that is not the case for everyone.

  I'm not suggesting that we start a program where middle and high school students get "nap time." What I am saying is that allowing students the opportunity to rest briefly during the day will positively impact their anxiety, emotional wellness, and productivity. For younger students, plan time in the day for quiet choice activities. Allow one of these choices to be a brief respite—an opportunity to lie down and close their eyes. Denote a corner of the classroom for this choice activity and play calming music for students who choose to take advantage of this time. For older students, build in time during the week for mindfulness meditation just before assessments or classwork, then dim the lights and lead them in relaxation. A power nap is usually fifteen minutes, but even providing students with five to ten minutes of rest for their minds can calm their emotions and recharge their bodies. A body that is well taken care of will result in a mind that is less anxious.

Who Doesn't Love a Snow Day?

It was March 21, 2018, and Boston was bracing for its fourth Nor'easter in as many weeks. What started as a quiet winter in 2017 was moving toward a dramatic one in 2018. As I sat and waited for the school closings to circle back around again, in the hopes of seeing my district listed, I couldn't help but feel the mix of excitement and anxiety that comes with the wonder of an unexpected day off.

My kids were thrilled. My oldest, a four-and-a-half-year-old, was running through the house playing hockey. My daughter, just over a year, was feeding off his exuberance.

"Mama, is it going to snow tonight?"

"Yes, buddy, it's going to snow."

"A lot?"

"Probably, Man Man."

"Are we going to have school?"

"I don't know, buddy, it's not likely."

"Yay!"

If only I could say that I felt the same way as he did.

Not surprisingly, the next day, the Boston area woke up to its fourth straight week with at least one snow day. It was a double-edged sword because with each new day off, I was getting additional rest, but I was also dealing with the increased anxiety that comes with another "Sunday." Sure, the night before was great: the excitement of not having to get up early, playing in the snow with the kids. But by midday, as the reality of having to think about going back to work after a day off set in, the anxiety that I felt on Sunday afternoons emerged with such intensity that the excitement of the storm was long gone.

Remember, anxiety is about control. Students with anxiety will worry the most about what they have the least control over. The reactions of others, the lessons planned by their teachers, and Mother Nature ... are completely out of the control of anxious students. Therefore, these circumstances are more anxiety-inducing than others.

We need to prepare for and anticipate the impact that days off will have on our students. If it changes a student's routine, it may be problematic for their emotional state in class. We can't control the weather, but we can set routines in place to ease into the first day back after time away. These routines can be minor and easy to implement. You can even maintain your planned lessons, as long as you compensate for the time away and get students reacquainted with the classroom. Help students regain control of their routines by focusing on a slow transition back to school.

LEAD **FORWARD** STRATEGY
Ease into the First Day Back

Students with anxiety need routine and structure, but every time a routine changes, they need time to adapt. The most obvious changes to their routines include the beginnings and ends of a vacation: summer, winter, and spring break. However, for students with anxiety, each weekend is a change in routine too. Sunday nights are especially difficult. Whether it's stomach ailments, sleepless nights, or irritability, anxiety will manifest itself for these students.

Unexpected days off can be even more difficult for students with anxiety; it's a change in routine without an opportunity to adjust to the idea ahead of time. The symptoms of their anxiety won't persist in anticipation; rather, they come on quickly and with increased intensity. This isn't the buildup of anxiety in the weeks leading to the start of a new school year, about which students and families can be proactive. Students can't account for sudden changes in routine, which can cause unmanageable and unpredictable panic attacks.

Educators can't prevent these reactions, but they can be sympathetic to what Sundays, snow days, and sick days mean for students with anxiety. Easing back into routines after unexpected time off is an effective support strategy.

- **Give students a menu of options during class.** Student voice is critical. It increases relevance and engagement for students and, in turn, increases productivity and success. Student-centered learning on the first day back from a weekend, snow day, or vacation helps ease students back into a routine. Yet it can also be overwhelming to students with anxiety. For example, I hate food shopping. Aside from the fact that there are other people to dodge and compete with, there are too many options. There is an entire aisle of salad dressing. If there were two, or even five, options, I could go down the aisle, pick one, and move on. That is not the case. Salad dressing selection can take ten minutes, on a good day.

This has resulted in complete avoidance. I either don't do the food shopping, or don't get salad dressing.

The same happens when you ask students with anxiety to pick what they want to do. They don't know where to start and end up avoiding the work altogether. Instead, give students a menu of options. On the first day back, make the lessons student-centered, but give the class a list of three to five options and let them choose what to do. This makes the transition smoother and eliminates work avoidance. A good first step is to start the first day back with some choice work. Allow students to pace themselves as they adjust back to the routine of school. Make this a habit, and it will become an expectation for students with anxiety. They will instantly feel in control of their return to school—which will instantly reduce their anxiety.

- **Be consistent.** The concept of easing back into school can be more straightforward than you think. Easing back refers to the performance demands you place on students. It doesn't mean easing back into classroom rules, expectations, or routines, because backing off on these can do more harm than good. Remember, the biggest need for these students is consistency. The operational and behavioral expectations of the classroom must never change.

The most impactful gift you can give to students with anxiety when routine changes is to be a reliable source of consistency. If snack time is from 9–9:30, stick to that time range, even if it's a "special day." If you give an inch, they'll take a mile, and for students with anxiety, every inch can negatively impact their emotions. Kids will test your limits and make it seem like they don't want to follow your expectations. But the reality is, kids thrive on structure. The same is true of our students with anxiety, especially when they are transitioning back from days off.

Start the first day back by reiterating the classroom rules and expectations; you can never be too transparent with your students, and the ones with anxiety will appreciate you for it.

- **Consider alternatives.** The beginning of the school year can be difficult for students, beyond the fears and anxieties of the first day. It takes a school quite some time to fall into a regular schedule. The onset of a new year is beset with school pictures, class assemblies, summer reading, orientations, fire drills, and safety trainings. To accommodate all of these bureaucratic necessities, school administrators alter the school's daily schedule. As a result, students miss certain classes while they sit in others for extended periods.

  Every day with another interruption is a day when students with anxiety will struggle to find consistency and routine. Rather than constantly changing schedules, consider implementing alternative schedules for the first few days of school. You'll ease students back into the routine of academia and also allow for the completion of the aforementioned tasks. Student anxiety will be diminished and expectations will be clear.

  In the fall of 2019, I scheduled the first two days of the school year so that all forms, surveys, pictures, assessments, orientations, exercises, and class introductions could take place on those days. This meant that there were no interruptions to the school schedule after that point. I found it not only successful, but preferred by students and staff. Staff were able to come in on the third day and just start teaching, and students with anxiety could spend two days getting used to the return to "school," while knowing that on day three, they could fall into their regular school routine.

MOVING FORWARD

Anxiety is about control. Situations that fall outside of their control make anxious students even more anxious. To counteract that anxiety, to extinguish those flames, students with anxiety become dependent on the expected and on the routine. Routines are comfortable and predictable. They provide time in which an anxious mind doesn't have to wonder. Sure, their thoughts are still busy, but they don't have to think about fears or doubts, or what's going to happen next.

We must model routine for students. Put together a consistent unit structure, use a weekly agenda rather than just a daily one, and structure your lessons with definitive objectives and activities both to open and close the lessons.

Remember that a healthy body leads to a healthy mind. Routines are important emotionally, but they are also necessary for the physiology of our bodies. Prioritize a healthy body in the classroom. Let students move, make sure they are well nourished, and give them the opportunity to rest their bodies and minds. Find times in your weekly agenda to devote to a healthy body in the classroom. Each of these need not take more than five to ten minutes. Helping students with anxiety get their bodies into a routine will help support their mental health too.

Ease into the days when you're returning from weekends, vacations, holidays, or snow days. Even one day out of school can throw off our students with anxiety. Give them choices for student-directed activities on the first days back by providing a list of potential options. Remember to maintain classroom expectations for structure and behavior. Maintain the established classroom routines because students crave consistency, even if they don't realize it.

Lastly, consider alternative schedules for the first days of the school year. Rather than constantly breaking the school's schedule over the first month to accommodate necessary beginning-of-the-year tasks, build special scheduling to get it all done and out of the way. It might require increased patience from teachers and staff, but it will allow for students with anxiety to adjust to the dramatic changes that come with a new school year, while being able to find comfort in their new routines much earlier in the year.

THINK **ABOUT** IT

1. What routines can you add to your schedule to benefit anxious students?

2. How can you help attend to the needs of your students' bodies, such as more time to move, or more time to rest?

3. Where in your school or classroom can you offer students a choice among options?

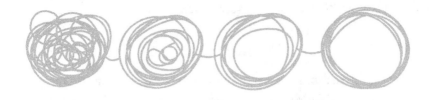

CHAPTER 10

Create Community

Encourage Extracurricular Activities and Non-Traditional Classrooms to Eliminate the Isolation of Anxiety

When I was young, my ambition was to be one of the people who made a difference in this world. My hope is to leave the world a little better for having been there.

— JIM HENSON, AMERICAN PUPPETEER AND PRODUCER

SUFFERING FROM ANXIETY can be lonely, and sufferers are often stuck inside of their own heads by themselves. Their mind, the illness, becomes their best friend. The isolation that anxiety creates functions as positive feedback. The more isolating it becomes, the more alone they want to be. The sooner educators can step in, the less time anxiety has to isolate its victim.

Educators need to find ways to help students with anxiety feel like they are part of a community that's bigger than themselves and their mental health. Create this sense of community in two ways: outside of the school day via extracurricular activities, i.e., athletics and clubs, or during the school day via the classroom experiences that educators create for their students.

Diving Right In

Jared was a freshman, a small kid with long hair, and only a few friends. He had suffered from anxiety for most of his childhood. What his mother thought was just a shy demeanor ended up being clinically diagnosed as anxiety. Not only was Jared unlikely to participate in class or be the center of attention among friends, but he was afraid to speak in front of his peers or initiate friendships.

Jared didn't dislike school. He had reasonably good grades and his attendance was fine. But Jared's mother was worried about his future. Would he continue to perform well academically? Would he find friends and have a social life? As it was, Jared simply came home from school and played video games until his mother got home from work. He was good about getting homework done after that, but his friends were online, not on demand.

Given all Jared's mom had come to know, but maybe not quite understand, about her son, she felt she had to get a bit aggressive to get him socially involved. She had given him the first six weeks of the new year to take the initiative and join a sports team or club, but, as expected, Jared had yet to do so. She had no interest in forcing his hand, but she was at a point where she felt Jared needed to see how much he could gain by stepping out of his comfort zone.

"Jared, I want you to start thinking about what you might like to do after school in the winter or spring," she said at dinner one night.

"What do you mean?" Jared asked in confusion.

"I mean you need to get involved in a club or a sport. Something. We talked about this over the summer, and you haven't done it yet."

"I don't really have any interest in anything, Mom."

"I get that, Jared. But I don't want you looking back on high school and regretting that you didn't get more involved. How about swimming?" She waited to see if he had a response. He didn't. "You always love being in the water. I can't get you out of the pool when you go to your Aunt Sally's house."

"That's not like real swimming, Mom."

"Real swimming? So, what, you need to be Michael Phelps or something?"

"Nooooo, Mom." Jared giggled. "But you can't be me."

"Why can't *you* be you, Jared? Will you try it? Please?"

"Mom." Jared was starting to get annoyed with his mother.

"Okay, fine. Go out for basketball, then. Or track."

"Basketball? Track?" Jared started laughing out loud. "Mom, you know as well as I do that I couldn't run or shoot a basketball if my life depended on it."

"Exactly. But you can swim."

After numerous threats by his mother to walk him into basketball tryouts or take his Xbox away—which Jared knew his mother would absolutely follow through with—he found himself standing on the pool deck, shirtless and in his summer bathing suit, listening to the coach give the team its first workout.

Five hundred SKIPS? What the hell are those?

"New members in lanes 1 and 2, everyone else, get in your usual lanes. Mini Me, can you jump in lane 1 or 2 and help the new folks?" the coach instructed.

"Sure, Coach!" Mini Me was the swim captain and the perfect mentor to younger kids. He joined the team as a freshman with little skill, and through hard work and commitment, became one of the coach's go-to swimmers. His nickname, Mini Me, was given to him by his coach, and it stuck.

"Come on, guys, grab a kickboard and pull buoy," Mini Me explained. "I'll tell you what you're going to do."

The first practice went well, and Jared enjoyed it. The swimming was harder than he expected, but he liked the coach and the rest of the team. He found the kids to be welcoming and the environment not too competitive. When he got home and told his mom about it, she was happy to hear he had fun.

"And they don't make cuts," he explained. "The team is small so everyone makes it. Of course, I might not compete, but that's okay."

That first practice didn't turn out to be an anomaly. After every practice, he liked swimming more than he had the day before. He had been correct that the team was small, and therefore the coach wasn't making cuts, but he was wrong about not competing. Jared had the opportunity to swim in B team relays, and toward the end of the season, he even got to swim in individual events. Even more important, he started socializing with the team outside of practice and meets. He went to team dinners and hung out with the team on weekends. He became a different person and even took to the nickname the team gave him: Minnow. He was the smallest member of the team and one of the worst swimmers. His teammates and coaches gave him the nickname, and it stuck.

Jared wasn't bothered by it; in fact, he loved it. It was a sign of affection, an acknowledgment that even though he was small and a bad swimmer, his teammates still loved him. As he continued to swim in his sophomore and junior years, the members who were younger than him didn't even know what his real name was. He was Minnow.

Jared began to soar in school. He loved the swim team so much that it became the basis of his entire social life in high school. His grades went up, his teachers talked about an outgoing and engaging student at parent/teacher conferences, and members of the girls' swim team even became his good friends.

The changes in Jared were not only apparent to his mom. Jared saw them too. The swim team made his high school experience amazing. It was so important to him that when the Athletic

Booster Club awarded him a varsity jacket at the end of his sophomore year, there was only one name he ever imagined displaying
proudly on his right shoulder: Minnow '10.

Jared's anxiety had become so familiar to him that it was a form
of comfort. Even if a situation is not good for us, if it's familiar, we
have a fear of letting it go, and it's the same with anxiety. Students
with anxiety are often crippled by their disease, much like Jared
was. Unfortunately, it's harder to fight it than educators realize. For
many students with anxiety, it's all they know. As controlling as it
is, it's predictable and routine, and they can bet on it. Change, even
for the better, can induce anxiety. Students might become overwhelmed at the idea of unscheduled time, and time without anxiety is exactly that. We must help students make the changes they
might know are beneficial, but are too afraid to make on their own.

LEAD **FORWARD** STRATEGY
Encourage Extracurricular Activities

Extracurricular activities are essential for students with anxiety.
Feeling like they are a part of a bigger picture and having an outlet
are great ways to cope. Encourage students to participate in activities outside of the classroom and within the greater school community. The more value they can place on themselves with activities
like that, the less control their anxiety will have over them.

Students with anxiety have minds that run wild, convincing them
they're not good enough or that no one is interested enough in what
they have to offer. Eventually, they decide it's easier just to be alone.
It's not worth the energy required to fight the self-doubt and fear,
when ultimately, they don't know if they're going to be accepted.

You also can't *see* anxiety. It's not as if you can sit in a classroom and pick out, just by looking at the students, the individuals who are suffering. It's true that you can't necessarily look at

someone and know they have diabetes, either, but perhaps you see them checking their blood sugar at the gym, or while shopping in the market. Maybe the student has to go to the nurse every day during the same class to get insulin. But with anxiety, there are no obvious identifiers.

When you have anxiety, you feel like it's just you and your illness. It's selfish and controlling. It wants the individual for itself and will come up with any reason or excuse, no matter how irrational it is, to achieve that. We need to help our students fight back, to normalize anxiety, and remove the shackles chained to their feet. Encourage students to get involved in extracurricular activities. It can be hard, but when it works, students can break the routine their anxiety has established and change the quiet loneliness upon which it feeds. Encourage students to engage in activities outside of the regular school day. It's easier than you might think.

- **Tell students that sports aren't about championships.**
  I played competitive sports through my twenties. For me, it was always about being the best and winning. I didn't play sports to socialize or meet new people. It wasn't about camaraderie or team dinners. I found it frustrating when teammates didn't seem to care when we lost. Bus rides home after a hard-fought loss were quiet and reflective for me, but for many of my teammates, they were extensions of school lunch: social hour filled with gossip and singing.

  This all changed for me in my first few years of teaching, when I became our school's freshman soccer coach. On the first day, when I asked the girls what positions they played, one looked at me with a blank stare, only to disclose moments later that she'd never played soccer. At that moment, I knew it wasn't going to be about winning. It was a bit of a transition for me, but the one game we did win that season (we were 1–15), was the closest I ever came to knowing what it would feel like to win a championship.

Students need to participate in sports for every reason I never did: camaraderie, companionship, exercise, and being part of a purpose outside of themselves. Even if they're not great at a sport (yet), they simply need to like it, much like Jared and swimming. In an article by Kashmira Gander that appeared in *Newsweek* on May 21, 2019, exercise was shown to ease the symptoms of anxiety and depression. The article cited a study from *Global Advances in Health and Medicine*, where one hundred individuals being treated for mental illness (specifically anxiety), depression, and anger, were subjected to a tailored exercise program. At the conclusion of the study, 95 percent of individuals said their mood had improved, and 63 percent said they were happy or very happy, rather than neutral, sad, or very sad.

Here's the science behind the results, according to the article: "Exercise appeared to help those with mental illness as it affects neurotransmitters like dopamine, noradrenaline, and serotonin, which are essential for stabilizing and improving mood disorders, but particularly depression anxiety." Sports gets students to move, and movement is scientifically good for anxiety.

Encourage students to try an activity at school, even if they aren't good at it. Talk to them about what they like to do and help them choose what would help them fit in the school community. Offer to take the student to meet the coach or a team member before the first tryout or practice.

- **Incorporate community service into the school day.** It's empowering to know you have helped someone else. As a sufferer of anxiety, I, like so many others, have coping mechanisms to which I can resort. Since co-founding a 501(c) nonprofit in June 2017, sitting down and completing work for my organization has become one of my go-to activities. The difference I feel I am making in the lives of others gives me a sense of purpose and shows my anxiety that I am capable.

  Incorporate community involvement and service in your school and classroom. You'll influence the school climate to form a new school culture and deepen the school-to-community connection that is so necessary in twenty-first-century teaching and learning. Community service work also gives students with anxiety an opportunity to get involved in an extracurricular activity to improve their self-worth and confidence. It empowers them by making a difference in the lives of others.

  The ultimate goal for students with anxiety is to provide them with a mental break from it. If you can incorporate self-talk that counters the voice of their anxiety, even better. Ask students if there is a cause that matters to them—a cause close to home. Tell the student that you will help them come up with an idea to support the cause. Start small. Suggest a way to educate others about the cause. You'll build a foundation for the student and begin to have a positive impact on the student's anxiety. These conversations may even lead to the next bullet point.

Image 10.1: Supporters of my nonprofit organization, Running from Anxiety, wearing our wristbands. Working for the organization has become a coping strategy for my anxiety.

Image 10.2: I'm passing out the cowbell medals to the finishers of our annual 5K run. Being there for the moment when others overcome is humbling and inspiring and helps me continue to fight my own anxiety.

- **Support new clubs.** Encourage students to join one of the many valuable clubs and offerings at school that extend beyond the realm of athletics. Students have found great purpose in drama, band, art, debate, science, gay-straight alliance, and foreign language clubs, to name a few. But the most impactful clubs I have seen are those that were proposed and founded by students: The Harry Potter Club, Answer for Cancer, A New Mentality, Anime Club, Magic Club, and D&D Club, just to name a few.

  Tell students they can start their own clubs in your building. I've heard so many students wonder what it would be like to have a club based on this or that, but their dreams die hard because they don't realize that they're allowed to create clubs of their own. Clubs offer students the opportunity to find an activity they enjoy and create a group with common interests. Doing so can help them normalize their mental illness. Empowering a student to establish a new club makes this even more impactful. The student owns the club and is responsible for its success—a control equal to or even more powerful than the control anxiety has over them. Once you find a cause a student is interested in, brainstorm with them what it might look like if there was a club at school to promote and support the cause. Show them the paperwork they need to complete. Offer to be the new club's advisor. Be a facilitator of the student's idea. It will help improve their self-worth and distract them from their anxiety.

Growing with Each Other

George was a veteran teacher who started his career as an aide before becoming a full-time teacher in the science department. From the students' perspective, he was likable, and from his colleagues' point of view, he was a talented teacher who was relatable and innovative.

A few years into his tenure, his classroom was moved from the science department to the career and technical education wing. This move allowed him easier access to the greenhouse for his botany class. That greenhouse, originally just a resource, quickly became the center of his curriculum. He'd intended to use the plants for experimentation only, but changed his mind after teaching the course for a single trimester. He was spending more time in the courtyard and greenhouse than in his classroom. He suffered from anxiety and found working in the greenhouse to be relaxing and calming. He was confident with his work, and more patient with his students during and after spending time in the greenhouse.

Not surprisingly, George's botany students, some of whom

opened up about their struggles with anxiety, felt the same way about the greenhouse. Being out of the confines of the classroom was soothing and reduced their anxiety. They felt like they could breathe and were more productive as a result. George wasn't surprised by these positive impacts, since doing yardwork at home had always been a coping strategy for him. But he was shocked to see how many of his students felt the same way. He decided to revamp his curriculum for the course to support even more work in the greenhouse, but he needed approval first.

He approached his department head to explain the diversion from what he originally proposed for the course.

"I have an idea for botany and I want to run it by you to make sure you're okay with it."

"Great, let's hear it," Caitlyn said enthusiastically.

"So, the kids are interested in working more in the greenhouse, and so am I. They're interested in it. They love being out there. They're productive, they are calm, and to be honest, the whole dynamic of the class is totally different. I also think I'm a better teacher."

"Really?"

"Yeah. I'm calm. I don't feel anxious. There's less pressure. The students are more engaged. In fact, a few of them talked about how much more relaxed they are when they're out there."

"Well, it sounds like it's good for everyone. Can you make the curriculum more relevant by using the greenhouse more?"

"Absolutely! I'm already teaching them about planting and fruits and vegetables. I had them choose a crop and do a project on it that included making a dish with the vegetables they've grown as an ingredient."

"And how'd that go over?" Caitlyn asked with a smile.

"It was good. The kids got into it and the food they made was delicious."

"Then I'm totally on board with it. I told you at the beginning of the year that I wanted you to take risks in the classroom; it's the only way you're going to grow as an educator. Some will work, and some won't. But how are you going to know if you don't try?"

"Awesome. I've been thinking about changing the whole trajectory of the class, to be honest. I think it should be more about planting and gardening."

"Yeah?" Caitlyn sounded a little skeptical this time. She might have wondered how George was planning to sell *that* class to teenagers?

"Yeah, so like a farm-to-table class. We could work out in the greenhouse and grow vegetables for the culinary program. They could let us know what they want, and we could harvest it for them."

George had been working the summer program for the last six years and was focusing his efforts on getting the students to beautify the school grounds. This work included planting vegetables in the greenhouse.

"Do you think the students would like that enough for it to be sustained as an entire course?"

"Caitlyn, I'm telling you, the students love being down there. I have kids that I can't get to do any work in class, and I take them to the greenhouse, and they're all in. I even informally asked the students why they thought that was, and they explained that the work doesn't make them anxious."

"George, go with it. You're a great teacher, and I trust you if you think this is the right direction. I'll support you however you need."

George went through with his plan to revamp the botany program with the support of his department head. He ended up rewriting the course as a co-taught elective with a teacher in the history department. The greenhouse became the epicenter of greater school-wide collaboration. Students in the class worked with special needs students in sub-separate classes to teach them how to plant, weed, water, and harvest in the greenhouse. They also devised programming with the students in the preschool and got the children into the greenhouse to work. They built raised garden beds outside the playground so they could grow fruits and vegetables. The students in the former botany class had become part of a group bigger than themselves. They were engaging with people of all ages and abilities to accomplish a common goal: learning the benefits and business of agriculture.

Image 10.3: One of the preschool students works in the greenhouse at Bowmen High School.

For George, the course was the only time during his workday in which he was anxiety-free. He never worried about evaluations or classroom management. Students in the course who expressed anxiety in their other classes said they looked forward to going to botany. The literal escape from the classroom became a figurative escape from anxiety.

LEAD **FORWARD** STRATEGY
Create Value in the Intracurricular

Educators need to find ways to implement intracurricular activities that feel more like extracurricular activities and result in the same emotional outcomes for students and staff. Let's make the concept of the classroom less literal. Any experience can be considered a "classroom." A greenhouse, a lab, or a field trip are all classrooms when in use. Take risks in changing your ideas of what a classroom is or should be. Anxiety excels in confined spaces, so we need to take ourselves, and our students, out of the restraints of the classroom. We need to introduce them to learning beyond the school walls.

Extracurricular activities are invaluable opportunities for students. They provide individuals with the chance to engage in activities that not only give them a break from their anxiety, but give them value and self-worth. But extracurricular activities shouldn't be the only place where students can meet these needs. There must be more inclusive opportunities for kids. This is not to say that extracurricular activities are inherently exclusive, but they can be. Often, participation in athletics or even performing arts requires user fees. Many students can't meet these financial requirements. In other cases, students have after-school obligations, like work or siblings, that prevent them from accessing extracurricular activities.

We must prioritize creating value in intracurricular activities as well. Self-worth, camaraderie, and inclusion can, and should, be part of the classroom experience for students with anxiety. When a curriculum is designed with student voice in mind and is made relevant to their lives, students are more likely to find freedom from anxiety. The botany course that George and his co-teacher designed accomplished this for students. They created a curriculum that reduced student (and teacher) anxiety by allowing students to find value in their peers, nature, and in those who weren't just like them. The greatest accomplishment of the course was the ability to redefine "normal" for students, both physically and emotionally. Accomplishing this occurs when educators do the following:

- **Establish non-traditional classrooms.** Too often, our twenty-first-century classrooms look like our 1950s classrooms. Students are seated in rows at individual desks, and the teacher is at the head of the class, dictating the lesson. The classroom is teacher-centered. Teachers assess students in a traditional manner and provide written quizzes and tests with multiple-choice, short answer, and essay-type questions. If there is any collaboration in the class, it is a suggestion or afterthought. "Work on these problems. If you want to pair up and work with a partner, feel free."

  These classrooms represent the experiences today's educators had when they were students. The structure worked back then because students were able to find success despite the lack of flexibility or creativity. Today, however, the students themselves are different.

  Students with anxiety need non-traditional classrooms that give them the opportunity to escape the four walls they stare at all day. George's classroom was anything but traditional. Students learned their greatest lessons in a greenhouse. The work they did with the preschool and special needs students was the most impactful to them. George designed an environment in which his students found a sense of purpose, togetherness, and selflessness that resulted in students with anxiety finding success emotionally and academically.

Start by committing to one day a week outside of the traditional classroom. If you can't find a physical space that is not a traditional classroom, *convert* the classroom into a less traditional space. In my classroom, I implemented Family Fridays. Every Friday, students were allowed to sit on the floor, on top of their desks, or in other furniture they brought into the classroom, e.g., separate chairs. The idea was to make ourselves more physically comfortable by removing the stuffiness of the classroom. Students said they were less anxious on Fridays, even if they were completing individual work. We created a sense of community in class on Fridays just by removing the confines of a desk. Educators can make small changes to create big impacts.

Implement intracurricular activities in the classroom to provide anxious students with the same camaraderie created by extracurricular activities. Try non-traditional classrooms, getting students involved in the greater school community, and participating in lessons yourself.

- **Work with the greater school community.** Getting students outside the confines of the traditional classroom is a great way to create more relevant learning experiences. However, meaningful learning happens when students can engage in the greater school community. Design lessons around the idea of giving back to provide students with the same self-worth as community service. Allowing a student with anxiety to help another individual quiets the struggle in their mind. Getting students to work in the greenhouse was meaningful and relaxing for George's students, but when George found ways to get his students to engage with the greater school community, he empowered and freed them from the mental bondage of their anxiety.

Think about a first date. The best advice you can give to someone going on a first date is to do an activity. Have an event other than yourselves be the center of attention. Sitting across from each other in a restaurant, trying to maintain a conversation for an hour or more, is stuffy, formal, and anxiety-inducing for anyone; never mind someone with clinical anxiety. For students with anxiety, this is how a classroom feels. And just like a first date, when you remove the part that causes anxiety—in this case, the confining structure of the environment—you get a more positive outcome. You get people being themselves without anxiety.

Collaborate with your colleagues. Come up with activities that your classes could engage in together. Ask students how they would like to engage a larger audience in their work. Let them dream big and then work with them to make it more realistic. Students could make guest presentations in other classes. They could organize an assembly or travel to another school to work with younger students on a lesson of their own. The classroom is where you meet; it isn't where the real learning occurs.

Image 10.4: Students in the Bowmen High School farm-to-table class used materials from the plumbing program to build grow tubes in the greenhouse. This learning environment helped all students strive, especially those with anxiety.

- **Participate as the teacher.** Getting students out of the classroom and working with other individuals in the community is essential to their confidence and social/emotional well-being. But if you want them to feel like what they're doing is valuable, you have to participate as well. If the work you are asking students to do is meaningful or is going to make them feel better about themselves, why aren't you doing it too?

  In exercise classes, the instructor is always participating. Zumba is not taught from the sidelines, and neither is truly meaningful teaching. Role models are doers. They become inspirations because of their actions, not their ideas.

  As educators, we've been taught that hands-on learning is the most powerful. So is hands-on teaching. We learn by doing, not watching. And we teach by doing, not assigning. When you participate with your students, you build positive relationships. Think of it like stooping down to the level of a student when you're answering a question at their desk. Participating in the lesson and learning brings you down to the level of the student. You also make students feel less alone when you participate. You rid the space of the isolation that comes from mental illness.

  The classroom is a unit, a family, and each of you plays a significant role in the healthy functioning of the entire organism. Whenever students presented their work in my class, I asked them to provide the audience with a task—and I performed that task as well. I would even let the presenters grade my work. The students loved it. This strategy is straightforward: If you're asking the students to do it, you should be too. Students with anxiety will feel more in control over their learning and less anxious if their teachers are also students.

MOVING **FORWARD**

Anxiety is isolating. Sufferers are in an abusive relationship with themselves, one where their significant other, their anxiety, is controlling, manipulative, and takes them away from the other people in their lives. Anxiety isn't physically abusive in all cases, but it's emotionally abusive enough that they will feel physically worn down.

Educators need to help students with anxiety feel less isolated. Through extracurricular activities, whether sports, community service, or other clubs, educators can provide students with anxiety the opportunity to find peers, or at least provide them with a sense of belonging and purpose that comes with being around others.

These activities can exist outside of the classroom too. Implement intracurricular activities in the classroom to provide anxious students with the same camaraderie created by extracurricular activities. Try non-traditional classrooms, getting students involved in the greater school community, and participating in lessons yourself, and you'll help your students free themselves from the abusive relationship controlled by anxiety.

THINK ABOUT IT

1. How can you encourage students to get more involved in the school and community?

2. How can you take risks and make your classroom less traditional?

3. How can you increase your own participation in your class?

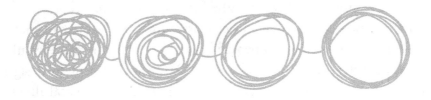

Conclusion

Everyone Has a Story to Tell

I'M SITTING IN the back of the classroom, leg shaking, manila folders on the table in front of me. The room is generic but brand new; it looks as sterile as a hospital room. The professor is at the front of the room engaging the class—nine students, all seated independently.

It's obvious I'm an outsider; they've met numerous times as a class already, and now they're looking at me and wondering, "Who's the new girl in the back of the room?" I'd rather just fade away. My choice of seats was an honest attempt at turning figurative speech into reality, but to no avail.

I'm a mix of emotions: excited, eager, nervous, nostalgic. It was just over a year ago that I was one of them: a student in this professor's class, hoping one day to earn my license and become an educational leader. It was then that I made an impactful connection with my professor. She'd heard about my nonprofit organization and needed to know more. As it turned out, she spent time working to educate individuals about mental illness in Greater Boston. She was looking for a teenager to present to the board of her organization that spring. I gave her my organization's information and the name of my co-founder, and we solidified the relationship.

Here I was again, back in her classroom. I was about to make my second presentation to her class, but this time, my grade would be quite different. What was previously an assignment to design my ideal school is now a guest lecture: my story of mental illness in schools, personally and professionally. The grade I would inevitably receive would mean more to me than any A, B, C, or D I'd ever gotten in the world of academia. This grade was personal: an assessment of the validity and delivery of *my* story. I had taught for fifteen years, stood in front of upward of fifty-five to sixty students at a time and delivered lessons and prompts, and shared snippets of my life. But those messages were presented to an audience that knew me, trusted me, and looked to me for answers.

As I sat in the back of this classroom on the campus of a state university, I felt like I was going to vomit; my heart was surely going to beat out of my chest. I was diving headfirst into the waters that would push me toward my dream: sharing my story with the world in hopes of helping those who are just like me and fighting anxiety every single day.

That day, I got up in front of the class and spoke for an hour. I told the class of nine, and my former professor, who I was, who I had been, and who I wanted to be. I stood in front of the room emotionally naked and profusely sweating. At the end of my presentation, I got a round of applause and heard from my professor that for their final projects, all nine students included mental health services as priorities in their ideal schools. I never received an actual grade for my presentation that day, of course, but I did receive emails from students, thanking me for coming, and another invite from my professor to speak down the road—all A's in my book.

Everyone has a story to tell. That's not to say any one person's story is more important or impactful than anyone else's. What it does mean is that you do not see who a person is. Mental illness doesn't have a face. It's often not recognizable to anyone, not even the individual who has it. When it does make an appearance, it often looks different each time, masked as yet another villain in that person's life. Educators need to be empathetic to students and their stories. They also need to tell their own stories, to be vulnerable and authentic. When educators find the courage to bring their stories into the classroom, they become role models to young people.

For many, this might be uncomfortable, but risk-taking is contagious. When educators show their students that the classroom is a place where lives come together with the stories of our lives, they succeed in normalizing the struggles of mental illness. When we deny the existence of the experiences that shape who our students are, we put up a roadblock to authentic teaching and learning.

Tell your story; communicate your why. Step out of your comfort zone and be an advocate for students with anxiety. Ask them questions, learn who they are. Learn the stories they bring to your classroom. Education is about lifelong learning for students *and* educators.

For me, my story is simple: I have a mental illness. I'm *Anxious*. Every day, I fight and take the risk to be the best version of myself I can be in an effort to empower those around me to take a risk too. Because it's not about "What if that risk goes wrong?" It's about "What if it turns out *right*?"

About the Author

Christine Ravesi-Weinstein is an avid writer and educator who is passionate about bridging the two with her mental health advocacy. She is the co-founder of the nonprofit organization Running from Anxiety. Currently, she is an assistant principal at a public high school in Massachusetts, and she previously served as a high school science department chair for four years and a classroom teacher for fifteen years. Christine earned her master's degree in education with a concentration in teaching and curriculum writing from Harvard University in June of 2003. Follow her on Twitter @RavesiWeinstein, read about her organization at runningfromanxiety.org, and learn more about her at ravesiweinstein.com.

Acknowledgments

I WOULD NEVER FIND myself writing the acknowledgments at the end of a book without the help of many people in my life. Given the pace at which life moves, it's unlikely that I will be able to provide all of the individual thank-you's here that I should include, but I will endeavor to do my best.

I have been fortunate to spend the last seventeen years of my life in education. I have come across and worked with more people than I can remember. So many of you have had a positive influence on my career as a teacher, administrator, and mental health advocate. To the students I have taught: Thank you for buying into my why and trusting my process. I only began to believe in myself as a leader and motivator when you became part of my #APBIOFamily.

To my colleagues over the years: Thank you for challenging my thinking and pushing me to be a better educator. Your support and suggestions allowed me to find my niche and have confidence in my craft.

Thank you to Ellen Ullman, the first person to take a risk on me. In February of 2019, I wrote an article about mental illness in schools and sent it her way. She had no obligation to read it or give me feedback, but she did, and I am forever grateful. Ellen decided to publish that article and it turned into numerous others. If not for her belief in the abilities of a young, raw, never-heard-from-before writer with a message to share about mental illness in schools, my career would never have become what it has.

Thank you also to Connie Hamilton and Mark Barnes. You both have been instrumental in my work. You've never stopped believing in me and my voice. Mark welcomed me into his world and trusted me to carry on the essence of this series. I am honored. Jennifer Jas and Carrie White-Parrish, thank you for your guidance and patience on this project. I have learned so much from your expertise.

I also would like to thank Rich Piergustavo. Thank you for being a fantastic colleague, a mentor, and a role model. You have encouraged me to be myself since day one, and you never fail to give me the perspective, and sometimes brutal honesty, that I need. Your laughter makes every situation, no matter how hard, more manageable.

Life with a mental illness is unpredictable. Some days are so dark, you can't see any light, and some days so bright, you forget a darkness ever existed. But the key to moving forward is never getting too high or low. Thank you to my friends and family for providing my mind with the stability it so desperately needs. To Nathan and Rory, you fill my heart with the love and purpose that gets me through the hard times. You are the true essence of happiness and my life's greatest work. To Ari, you've been on this road trip with me since April of 2005 when we first took the coupe to the capitol. Thank you for letting me live my passions and for taking this ride with me; none of this would have been possible without you.

Life is full of decisions and choices, and that never changes. And being anxious makes those decisions and choices even more difficult. Regardless, you're only going to know which decision is the right one if you try. So go ahead, take the risk, and remind yourself: What if it turns out *right*?

More from
TIMES 10

Browse all titles at 10Publications.com

Hacking School Discipline:
9 Ways to Create a Culture of Empathy & Responsibility Using Restorative Justice
By Nathan Maynard and Brad Weinstein

Reviewers proclaim Washington Post Bestseller *Hacking School Discipline* to be "maybe the most important book a teacher can read, a must for all educators, fabulous, a game changer!" In a book that should become your new blueprint for school discipline, teachers, presenters, and school leaders Nathan Maynard and Brad Weinstein demonstrate how to eliminate punishment and build a culture of responsible students and independent learners. **Twelve straight months at #1** on Amazon and still going strong, HSD is disrupting education like nothing teachers and school leaders have seen in decades—maybe centuries.

Hacking Education:
10 Quick Fixes For Every School
By Mark Barnes and Jennifer Gonzalez

In this award-winning first Hack Learning Series book, Mark Barnes and Jennifer Gonzalez employ decades of teaching experience and hundreds of discussions with education thought leaders to show you how to find and hone the quick fixes that every school and classroom need. Using a Hacker's mentality, they provide one Aha moment after another with 10 quick fixes for every school—solutions to everyday problems and teaching methods that any teacher or administrator can implement immediately.

Browse all titles at 10Publications.com

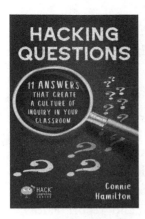

Hacking Questions:
11 Answers that Create a Culture of Inquiry in Your Classroom
By Connie Hamilton

Questions are the driving force of learning in classrooms. *Hacking Questions* digs into framing, delivering, and maximizing questions in the classroom to keep students engaged in learning. Known in education circles as the "Questioning Guru," Connie Hamilton shows teachers of all subjects and grades how to ask the questions that deliver not just answers but reflection, metacognition, and real learning.

Hacking Project Based Learning:
10 Easy Steps to PBL and Inquiry in the Classroom
By Ross Cooper and Erin Murphy

As questions and mysteries around PBL and inquiry continue to swirl, experienced classroom teachers and school administrators Ross Cooper and Erin Murphy wrote a book that empowers those intimidated by PBL to cry, "I can do this!" while providing added value for those who are already familiar with the process. *Hacking Project Based Learning* demystifies what PBL is all about with 10 hacks that construct a simple path that educators and students can easily follow to achieve success.

Browse all titles at 10Publications.com

Hacking Assessment:
10 Ways To Go Gradeless In a Traditional Grades School
By Starr Sackstein

In the bestselling *Hacking Assessment,* award-winning teacher and world-renowned formative assessment expert Starr Sackstein unravels one of education's oldest mysteries: How to assess learning without grades—even in a school that uses numbers, letters, GPAs, and report cards. While many educators can only muse about the possibility of a world without grades, teachers like Sackstein are reimagining education. This book shows you exactly how to create a remarkable no-grades classroom, a vibrant place where students grow, share, thrive, and become independent learners who never ask, "What's this worth?"

Hacking Leadership:
10 Ways Great Leaders Inspire Learning That Teachers, Students, and Parents Love
By Joe Sanfelippo and Tony Sinanis

In the runaway bestseller *Hacking Leadership*, renowned school leaders Joe Sanfelippo and Tony Sinanis bring readers inside schools that few stakeholders have ever seen—places where students not only come first, but have a unique voice in teaching and learning. The authors ignore the bureaucracy that stifles many leaders, focusing instead on building a culture of **engagement, transparency, and most importantly, fun**. *Hacking Leadership* has superintendents, principals, and teachers around the world employing strategies they never before believed possible.

Browse all titles at 10Publications.com

Anxious:
How to Advocate for Students with Anxiety, Because What If It Turns Out Right?
By Christine Ravesi-Weinstein

Clinical anxiety is on the rise, and educators are seeing more students struggling with the pressures of school and society. Whether you have anxiety or want to advocate for others, *Anxious* will change your thinking and encourage you to take risks in the classroom, and always ask, "What if it turns out right?" Christine Ravesi-Weinstein shares stories and strategies to help you advocate for anxious students. From her own experience as a teacher and administrator and someone with anxiety, she shows you how to recognize when anxiety causes students to avoid assignments and skip class; build relationships by asking questions first; help students understand the body-mind connection and become self-advocates; and create safe environments with authenticity, vulnerability, and routines.

Hacking School Culture:
Designing Compassionate Classrooms
By Angela Stockman and Ellen Feig Gray

Bullying prevention and character-building programs are deepening our awareness of how today's kids struggle and how we might help, but many agree: They aren't enough to create school cultures where students and staff flourish. This inspired Angela Stockman and Ellen Feig Gray to seek out systems and educators who were getting things right, and share their findings in this insightful book.

Browse all titles at 10Publications.com

Be Excellent on Purpose:
Intentional Strategies for Impactful Leadership
By Sanée Bell

Excellence is a journey where one discovers who they are, what they value, and the principles that drive them. Pursuers of excellence can see barriers as obstacles that they can overcome, and those barriers and challenges strengthen them in their pursuit of excellence. To *Be Excellent on Purpose* means not making excuses but making a plan for life and working the plan to make it a reality. Longtime teacher, author, presenter, and school leader Sanée Bell shares personal and professional stories and strategies that will make your leadership intentional and impactful, in this inaugural book in this revolutionary new leadership series.

Hacking Early Learning:
10 Building Blocks to Success in Pre-K–3 That All Teachers and School Leaders Should Know
By Jessica Cabeen

School readiness, closing achievement gaps, partnering with families, and innovative learning are just a few of the reasons the early learning years are the most critical in a child's life.

In *Hacking Early Learning*, kindergarten school leader, early childhood education specialist, and Minnesota State Principal of the Year Jessica Cabeen provides strategies for teachers, principals, and district administrators for best practices in preschool through third grade, including connecting these strategies to all grade levels.

Browse all titles at 10Publications.com

Hacking Engagement:
50 Tips & Tools to Engage
Teachers and Learners Daily
By James Alan Sturtevant

Unlike other education books that weigh you down with archaic research and impossible-to-implement strategies, *Hacking Engagement* provides 50 unique, exciting, and actionable tips and tools that you can apply right now. Try one of these amazing engagement strategies tomorrow: engage the enraged, create celebrity couple nicknames, hash out a hashtag, avoid the war on yoga pants, let your freak flag fly, become a proponent of the exponent, and transform your class into a focus group. Are you ready to engage?

Hacking Engagement Again:
50 Teacher Tools that Will Make
Students Love Your Class
By James Alan Sturtevant

Fifty student engagement hacks just weren't enough. Veteran educator and wildly popular student engager James Alan Sturtevant wowed teachers with his original book, *Hacking Engagement*. Those educators and students improved, and they craved more. So, Sturtevant created 50 more teacher tools that will make students love your class in *Hacking Engagement Again!*

Browse all titles at 10Publications.com

Quit Point:
Understanding Apathy, Engagement, and Motivation in the Classroom
By Adam Chamberlin and Svetoslav Matejic

In *Quit Point*, authors Chamberlin and Matejic present a new way of approaching the Quit Point—their theory on how, why, and when people quit and how to stop quitting before it happens. Their insights will transform how teachers reach the potential of every student. *Quit Point* reveals how to confront apathy and build student engagement, how to differentiate learning for all levels, interventions to challenge students to keep going, and applications and toolkits to help you address the Quit Point, starting tomorrow.

Hacking Digital Learning Strategies:
10 Ways to Launch EdTech Missions in Your Classroom
By Shelly Sanchez Terrell

International EdTech presenter and NAPW Woman of the Year Shelly Sanchez Terrell demonstrates the power of EdTech Missions—lessons and projects that inspire learners to use web tools and social media to innovate, research, collaborate, problem-solve, campaign, crowdfund, crowdsource, and publish. Included in the book is a 38-page Mission Toolkit, complete with reproducible mission cards, badges, polls, and other handouts that you can copy and distribute to students immediately.

Browse all titles at 10Publications.com

Hacking Classroom Management:
10 Ideas To Help You Become the Type of Teacher They Make Movies About
By Mike Roberts

Learn the 10 ideas you can use today to create the classroom any great movie teacher would love. Utah English Teacher of the Year and sought-after speaker Mike Roberts brings you quick and easy classroom management hacks that will make your classroom the place to be for all your students. He shows you how to create an amazing learning environment that makes discipline, rules, and consequences obsolete, no matter if you're a new teacher or a 30-year veteran teacher.

Quiet Kids Count:
Unleashing the True Potential of Introverts
By Chrissy Romano Arrabito

No matter what grade level or content you teach, you will have them sitting in your room: the introverts, the quiet kids, and the not-so-quiet, but introverts just the same. They don't cause trouble, and for the most part, they earn good grades. But these are the kids who tend to fade into the background and slip through the cracks. The ones who are so often overlooked or misunderstood. In this second Lead Forward Series book, author Chrissy Romano Arrabito provides a guidebook to help you better understand *all* types of introverts, allay the misconceptions, and to provide useful tips and strategies to help these students reach their full potential. *Quiet Kids Count* is a call to action for educators to step up and meet the needs of ALL learners— not just the ones that command the most attention.

Browse all titles at 10Publications.com

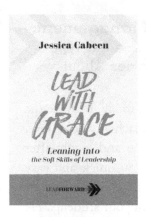

Lead with Grace:
Leaning Into the Soft Skills of Leadership
By Jessica Cabeen

With technology, we interact with families, students, and staff 24/7, not just during the school day or working hours. Pressures and demands at work can sway who we are and how we do it into a personality that favors more online likes than the authentic interactions we need to establish deep relationships with the students we serve. So, we need grace more than ever. Throughout this book, you'll read stories and strategies that will allow you to walk away with key practices and exercises that will build confidence so you can extend grace with others. School leader, author, and keynote speaker Jessica Cabeen provides frames that will empower anyone—teacher, principal, parent, or superintendent—to lead with grace.

Hacking the Writing Workshop:
Redesign with Making in Mind
By Angela Stockman

Agility matters. This is what Angela Stockman learned when she left the classroom over a decade ago to begin supporting young writers and their teachers in schools. What she learned transformed her practice and led to the publication of her primer on this topic: *Make Writing: 5 Teaching Strategies that Turn Writer's Workshop Into a Maker Space*. Now, Angela is back with more stories from the road and plenty of new thinking to share.

Browse all titles at 10Publications.com

Chasing Greatness:
26.2 Ways Teaching Is Like Running a Marathon
By Mike Roberts

After twenty years of teaching and more than fifty marathons, Mike Roberts is still chasing greatness. Now, he shares his experiences, while showing you, teacher and/or marathoner, how to run the most enriching race of your life.

Modern Mentor:
Reimagining Mentorship in Education
By Suzy Brooks and Matthew X. Joseph

As modern mentors, how can we shift our practices as individuals or make widespread change happen in our systems? Mentoring is not just checking a box; it is the process of developing colleagues who eventually work alongside us in a challenging profession where collaboration, connection, and consistency are vital for our students. This book showcases ways to develop mentoring programs, designed to assist teachers in becoming strong mentors and to assist new teachers in getting the most out of their mentoring relationship. Veteran educators, recognized school leaders, and expert mentors Suzy Brooks and Matthew X. Joseph bring you the stories and strategies that turn novice educators into EduStars.

Browse all titles at 10Publications.com

The Startup Teacher:

The Professional Learning Playbook Your Students Need You To Read … And You Deserve

By Michelle Blanchet and Darcy Bakkegard

The world is changing fast, and education hasn't caught up. Teachers know schools need more innovation, change-making, and relevance. But HOW? Authors Blanchet and Bakkegard grew tired of everyone telling teachers what to fix without sharing the "how," so they developed easy-to-use professional development tools and strategies to help teachers think like startup entrepreneurs. Using a visual, interactive format, *The Startup Teacher* helps teachers tackle challenges, turn their ideas into action, and tap into their potential to lead change in the classroom, school, and community. This book reveals how to evolve your teaching and learning to serve the changing needs of students, use professional learning and meeting time to break down challenges and create solutions, and cultivate your leadership capacity to take your ideas further than you ever imagined.

Hacking Homework:

10 Strategies that Inspire Learning Outside the Classroom

By Starr Sackstein and Connie Hamilton

Learning outside the classroom is being reimagined, and student engagement is better than ever. World-renowned author/educator Starr Sackstein has changed how teachers around the world look at traditional grades. Now she's teaming with veteran educator, curriculum director, and national presenter Connie Hamilton to bring you 10 powerful strategies for teachers and parents that inspire independent learning at home, without punishments or low grades.

Browse all titles at 10Publications.com

Make Writing:
5 Teaching Strategies That Turn Writers Workshop Into a Maker Space
By Angela Stockman

Everyone's favorite education blogger and writing coach, Angela Stockman, turns teaching strategies and practices upside down. She spills you out of your chair, shreds your lined paper, and launches you and your writer's workshop into the maker space! Stockman provides five right-now writing strategies that reinvent instruction and inspire both young and adult writers to express ideas with tools that have rarely, if ever, been considered. *Make Writing* is a fast-paced journey inside Stockman's Western New York Young Writer's Studio, alongside the students who learn how to write and how to make, employing Stockman's unique teaching methods.

Hacking Mathematics:
10 Problems that Need Solving
By Denis Sheeran

What if every one of your students loved math? Now, you can make the impossible a reality, and your students will race to complete your math problems. In *Hacking Mathematics*, teacher, author, and math consultant Denis Sheeran shows you how to hack your instructional approach and assessment procedures to promote an amazing culture of mathematical inquiry and engagement that few students ever see.

Browse all titles at 10Publications.com

Hacking School Libraries:
10 Ways to Incorporate Library Media Centers Into Your Learning Community
By Kristina A. Holzweiss and Stony Evans

In *Hacking School Libraries*, 2015 School Librarian of the Year Kristina A. Holzweiss, and 2017 Sensational Student Voice Award finalist Stony Evans bring you 10 practical hacks that will help you create a welcoming and exciting school library program. They show you how to rethink your library to become the hub of the school community, whether you are a veteran librarian or just beginning your career.

Hacking Instructional Design:
33 Extraordinary Ways to Create a Contemporary Curriculum
By Michael Fisher and Elizabeth Fisher

Whether you want to make subtle changes to your instructional design or turn it on its head— *Hacking Instructional Design* provides a toolbox of options. Discover just-in-time tools to design, upgrade, or adapt your teaching strategies, lesson plans, and unit plans. These strategies offer you the power and permission to be the designer, not the recipient, of a contemporary curriculum. Students and teachers will benefit for years to come when you apply these engaging tools starting tomorrow.

Browse all titles at 10Publications.com

Resources from Times 10

10Publications.com

**Join the Times 10 Ambassadors
and help us revolutionize education:**
10Publications.com/ambassador

Podcasts:
hacklearningpodcast.com
jamesalansturtevant.com/podcast

On Twitter:
@10Publications
@HackMyLearning
#Times10News
@LeadForward2
#LeadForward
#HackLearning
#HackingLeadership
#MakeWriting
#HackingQs
#HackingSchoolDiscipline
#LeadWithGrace
#QuietKidsCount
#ModernMentor
#AnxiousBook

All things Times 10:
10Publications.com

Vision, Experience, Action
10PUBLICATIONS.COM

TIMES 10 is helping all education stakeholders improve every aspect of teaching and learning. We are committed to solving big problems with simple ideas. We bring you content from experts, shared through books, podcasts, and an array of social networks. Our books bring Vision, Experience, and Action to educators around the world. Stay in touch with us at 10Publications.com and follow our updates on Twitter @10Publications and #Times10News.